Redux

An A-to-Z Walkthrough of the Most Important JavaScript State Management Library

By: Chong Lip Phang

Email:
webcodingbible@gmail.com

Souce Codes:
https://drive.google.com/file/d/16_EBnoG5QssDVIzJnapp0sPsZEzKYyEh/view?usp=sharing

Publisher:
Chong Lip Phang
Email: webcodingbible@gmail.com

Imprint: Independently published Chong Lip Phang, 1982-
XML. A Quick Guide to All Aspects.
By: Chong Lip Phang
ISBN: 9798371139597
1. Web sites – Design. 2. Online authorship.   I. Title. 006.7

Printed by:
Kindle Direct Publishing

Preface

Redux is an advanced JavaScript topic. Readers of this book are assumed to have prior knowledge of JavaScript and a JavaScript framework such as React.

Helping you manage shared "global" states across the various parts of your application, Redux is a library that can be used with any UI layer or framework, including React, Angular, Vue, Ember, and Vanilla JS.

Newcomers often ask why we cannot just use localStorage to manage all the states. The answers are:
- Using Redux alongside react-redux will help you correctly and conveniently re-render the components listening to the different states.
- Redux makes sure your components are in synchronization with your application states.
- localStorage can only store strings. Repeatedly stringifying/parsing localStorage will make your app slower and less responsive.
- localStorage persists across browser sessions. So, if you use it instead of Redux, you may need to manually delete some data to minimize disk usage.

You may not need Redux for small applications. However, for complex applications, the benefits of using Redux become apparent. After you have some real experience with React, you will see whether Redux is helpful for you. If you start directly with Redux, you may end up with over-engineered code that is harder to maintain, and with even more bugs.

For the sake of completeness and clarity, this book starts by showing the legacy method of using Redux, which is to include the Redux library directly in the HTML file. However, for modern real-world applications, you should be using Redux Toolkit (configureStore(), etc.) and pre-compile all the source files with a package manager such as 'create-react-app'.

Most source codes in this book have a corresponding version on CodeSandbox, links of which can be found within the public zip file on Google Drive (see URL at the beginning of this book). Readers are encouraged to run and experiment with the codes to gain a solid understanding of the concepts of Redux.

The last chapter of this book, Chapter 5: Ecosystem, is the direct adoption of a page of the official documentation. With due respect to the original writers, it is pointless to amend skillful writing.

Have fun managing application states!

Table of Contents

1. Basics

If you do not want to use a preprocessor like webpack, you can include the Redux library directly in your HTML file.

```
<script src="https://unpkg.com/redux@latest/dist/redux.min.js"></script>
```

1.1. Basic Usage

For every redux application, there should be exactly one data store.

To create the **store**, pass to createStore() a **reducer** function, which takes as parameters a **state** and an **action** object with a 'type' key.

Below we include the redux library directly in our HTML file, doing away with the need for any preprocessing (eg. using webpack).

```html
<!DOCTYPE html>
<html>
  <head>
    <title>Redux basic example</title>
    <script src="https://unpkg.com/redux@latest/dist/redux.min.js"></script>
  </head>
  <body>
    <div>
      <p>
        Clicked: <span id="value">0</span> times
        <button onclick="store.dispatch({ type: 'INCREMENT' })">+</button>
        <button onclick="store.dispatch({ type: 'DECREMENT' })">-</button>
      </p>
    </div>
    <script>
      function counter(state, action) {   // a reducer
        if (typeof state === 'undefined') return 0;
        switch (action.type) {
          case 'INCREMENT': return state + 1;
          case 'DECREMENT': return state - 1;
          default:       return state;
        }
      }
      var store = Redux.createStore(counter);
      function render() {
        document.getElementById('value').innerHTML = store.getState().toString();
      }
      render();
      store.subscribe(render);
    </script>
  </body>
</html>
```

Clicked: 0 times [+] [-]

After we have created our Redux store, we can:
- get the state of the store with *store.getState()*.
- update the state of the store with *store.dispatch(action)*.
- subscribe an event listener with *store.subscribe(listener)*, to be invoked every time *after* an action has been dispatched to the store.
- replace the reducer with *store.replaceReducer(newReducer)*.

To facilitate the dispatching of actions, you can define action creators, which are functions that return an action object:

```
function increment(){return {type:'INCREMENT'};}
function decrement(){return {type:'DECREMENT'};}
store.dispatch(increment());
```

You can further do away with calling dispatch() altogether by using bindActionCreators(). This is especially helpful if you wish to hide Redux:

```
function increment(){return {type:'INCREMENT'};}
function decrement(){return {type:'DECREMENT'};}
const inc = Redux.bindActionCreators(inc, store.dispatch);
const dec = Redux.bindActionCreators(dec, store.dispatch);
inc();
dec();
/* alternatively:
const ops = Redux.bindActionCreators({inc, dec}, store.dispatch);
ops.inc();
ops.dec();
*/
```

Note that createStore() can take a second parameter that initializes the state of the store, and/or an additional enhancer parameter which represents a list of functions to be called every time before dispatch() is called (eg. middleware):

```
const reducer = combineReducers({todos, visibilityFilter})
const initializer = {list:[0]};
const enhancer = compose(applyMiddleware(thunk), DevTools.instrument());

const store = createStore(reducer, initializer, enhancer);
```

Reducers can be combined with the combineReducers() function.

Enhancers can be combined with the compose() function.

As opposed to subscribers which are invoked *after* every dispatch event, middleware functions are invoked *before* every dispatch event. You can pass an enhancer without passing an initializer too:

```
const store = createStore(
 todoApp,
 applyMiddleware(
  rafScheduler,
  timeoutScheduler,
  thunk,
  vanillaPromise,
  readyStatePromise,
  logger,
  crashReporter
 )
)
```

You can 'spread out' your middleware if all pieces of your middleware are 'pushed' into an array:

```
applyMiddleware(...middleware)
```

1.2. Combining Reducers

As each reducer is associated with only one state, combining reducers allows you to have 'multiple states' in the Redux store.

Notice a store can subscribe to multiple listeners, which will be invoked in the order they are subscribed to every time an action is dispatched. Below, we can also render both X and Y within one function.

```html
<!DOCTYPE html>
<html>
  <head>
    <title>Redux basic example</title>
    <script src="https://unpkg.com/redux@latest/dist/redux.min.js"></script>
  </head>
  <body>
    <div>
      <p>
        <span id="valueX">0</span> / <span id="valueY">2</span>
        <button onclick="store.dispatch({ type: 'INCREMENT' })">+</button>
        <button onclick="store.dispatch({ type: 'DECREMENT' })">-</button>
        <button onclick="store.dispatch({ type: 'MUL', n:2 })">*2</button>
        <button onclick="store.dispatch({ type: 'MUL', n:3 })">*3</button>
        <button onclick="store.dispatch({ type: 'POW', n:2 })">^2</button>
        <button onclick="store.dispatch({ type: 'POW', n:3 })">^3</button>
      </p>
    </div>
    <script>
      function counter(state=0, action) {   // a reducer
        if (typeof state === 'undefined') return 0;
        switch (action.type) {
          case 'INCREMENT': return state + 1;
          case 'DECREMENT': return state - 1;
          default:        return state;
        }
      }
      function mfunc(state=2, action){   // another reducer
        switch (action.type) {
          case 'POW': return state ** action.n;
          case 'MUL': return state * action.n;
          default   : return state;
        }
      }
      var store = Redux.createStore(Redux.combineReducers({x:counter, y:mfunc}));
      function renderX() {
        document.getElementById('valueX').innerHTML = store.getState().x;
      }
      function renderY(){
        document.getElementById('valueY').innerHTML = store.getState().y;
      }
      renderX(); store.subscribe(renderX);
      renderY(); store.subscribe(renderY);
    </script>
  </body>
</html>
```

```
0 / 2  [ + ] [ - ] [ *2 ] [ *3 ] [ ^2 ] [ ^3 ]
```

Note that you can use the ES6 shorthand syntax

   Redux.combineReducers({counter, mfunc});

which is equivalent to:

   Redux.combineReducers({counter:counter, mfunc:mfunc});

3

1.3. applyMiddleware()

The middleware represents a set of functions that are automatically invoked *before* every dispatched action.

In contrast, subscribers are invoked *after* every dispatched action.

The middleware signature is
>   **({ getState, dispatch }) => next => action**

next(action), when invoking the reducer at the last stage of the pipeline, returns the action itself, and not the updated state. The call is synchronous.

```
<!DOCTYPE html>
<html>
  <head>
    <script src="https://unpkg.com/redux@latest/dist/redux.min.js"></script>
  </head>
  <body>
    <button onclick="store.dispatch({type: 'multiply', factor: 10})">Dispatch</button>
    <script>
      const reducer = (state, action) => {
        alert(state);
        return (action.type=="multiply") ? state * action.factor : state;
      };
      const alerter = ({ getState }) => next => action => {
        alert(getState()+" ...before");
        const v = getState() * next(action).factor;
        alert(v+" ...after");
        return action;
      };
      const store = Redux.createStore(reducer, 1, Redux.applyMiddleware(alerter, alerter));
    </script>
  </body>
</html>
```

| Dispatch |

1.4. compose()

compose() is used when you want to pass multiple store enhancers to the store.
Store enhancers are higher-order functions that add some extra functionality to the store. The only store enhancer which is supplied with Redux by default is applyMiddleware(). However, many others are available, eg. DevTools.

This example is identical to the previous one

```
<!DOCTYPE html>
<html>
  <head>
    <script src="https://unpkg.com/redux@latest/dist/redux.min.js"></script>
  </head>
  <body>
    <button onclick="store.dispatch({type: 'multiply', factor: 10})">Dispatch</button>
    <script>
      const reducer = (state, action) => {
        alert(state);
        return (action.type=="multiply") ? state * action.factor : state;
      };
      const alerter = ({ getState }) => next => action => {
        alert(getState()+" ...before");
        const v = getState() * next(action).factor;
        alert(v+" ...after");
        return action;
      };
      const store = Redux.createStore(reducer, 1, Redux.compose(
                                      Redux.applyMiddleware(alerter),
                                      Redux.applyMiddleware(alerter)));

    </script>
  </body>
</html>
```

Dispatch

1.5. Thunk

So far all our Redux operations have been synchronous.

Some actions, such as data fetching requests, are generally asynchronous in nature and warrant the use of thunks for an elegant coding pattern.

Redux Thunk is a middleware that lets you call action creators that return a function instead of an action object. That function receives the store's dispatch method, which is then used to dispatch regular synchronous actions inside the function's body once the asynchronous operations have been completed.

When the ReduxThunk middleware sees the action dispatched is a function, it invokes the function, which accepts the dispatch function as the first parameter.

```html
<!DOCTYPE html><html>
  <head>
    <title>Redux basic example</title>
    <script src="https://unpkg.com/redux@latest/dist/redux.min.js"></script>
    <script src=
     "https://cdnjs.cloudflare.com/ajax/libs/redux-thunk/2.4.1/redux-thunk.min.js">
    </script>
  </head>
  <body>
    <div>
      <p>
        Clicked: <span id="value">0</span> times
        <button onclick="store.dispatch(delayed_increment(2))">delayed +</button>
        <button onclick="store.dispatch(increment())">+</button>
      </p>
    </div>
    <script>
      function counter(state, action) {   // a reducer
        if (typeof state === 'undefined') return 0;
        switch (action.type) {
          case 'INCREMENT': return state + 1;
          case 'DECREMENT': return state - 1;
          default:          return state;
        }
      }
      function increment(){    // an action creator
        return {type:'INCREMENT'};
      }
      function delay(sec){    // an asynchronous operation
        return new Promise(resolve=>{
          setTimeout(resolve,sec*1000);
        });
      }
      function delayed_increment(sec){  // a thunk
        return function (dispatch, getState){
          delay(sec).then(()=>dispatch({type:'INCREMENT'}));
        }
      }
      var store = Redux.createStore(counter, Redux.applyMiddleware(ReduxThunk));
      function render() {
        document.getElementById('value').innerHTML = store.getState().toString();
      }
      render();
      store.subscribe(render);
    </script>
  </body></html>
```

The ReduxThunk middleware can accept an extra parameter.

```html
<!DOCTYPE html>
<html>
  <head>
    <title>Redux basic example</title>
    <script src="https://unpkg.com/redux@latest/dist/redux.min.js"></script>
    <script src="https://cdnjs.cloudflare.com/ajax/libs/redux-thunk/2.4.1/redux-thunk.min.js">
    </script>
  </head>
  <body>
    <div>
      <p>
        Clicked: <span id="value">0</span> times
        <button onclick="store.dispatch(delayed_increment(2))">delayed +</button>
        <button onclick="store.dispatch(increment())">+</button>
      </p>
    </div>
    <script>
      function counter(state, action) {   // a reducer
        if (typeof state === 'undefined') return 0;
        switch (action.type) {
          case 'INCREMENT': return state + 1;
          case 'DECREMENT': return state - 1;
          default:                return state;
        }
      }
      function increment(){    // an action creator
        return {type:'INCREMENT'};
      }
      function delay(sec){    // an asynchronous operation
        return new Promise(resolve=>{
          setTimeout(resolve,sec*1000);
        });
      }
      function delayed_increment(sec){   // a thunk
        return function (dispatch, getState, extraArg){
          delay(sec*extraArg).then(()=>dispatch({type:'INCREMENT'}));
        }
      }
      var store = Redux.createStore(counter,
                         Redux.applyMiddleware(ReduxThunk.withExtraArgument(3)));
      function render() {
        document.getElementById('value').innerHTML = store.getState().toString();
      }
      render();
      store.subscribe(render);
    </script>
  </body>
</html>
```

Clicked: 0 times [delayed +] [+]

The benefit of using middleware like Redux Thunk or Redux Promise is that components aren't aware of how action creators are implemented, whether they care about Redux state, whether they are synchronous or asynchronous, and whether they call other action creators.

1.6. DevTools

For Chrome, first, install Redux DevTools from Chrome Web Store.

```
<!DOCTYPE html>
<html>
  <head>
    <script src="https://unpkg.com/redux@latest/dist/redux.min.js"></script>
  </head>
  <body>
    <button onclick="store.dispatch({type: 'multiply', factor: 10})">Dispatch</button>
    <script>
      const reducer = (state, action) => {
        return (action.type=="multiply") ? state * action.factor : state;
      };
      const alerter = ({ getState }) => next => action => {
        const v = getState() * next(action).factor;
        alert(v+" ...after");
        return action;
      };
      const store = Redux.createStore(reducer, 1, Redux.compose(
                            Redux.applyMiddleware(alerter, alerter),
                            window.__REDUX_DEVTOOLS_EXTENSION__ &&
                            window.__REDUX_DEVTOOLS_EXTENSION__()));
    </script>
  </body>
</html>
```

Dispatch

| □ □ | Elements | Console | Sources | Network | Performance | Memory | Application | Security | Lighthouse | Recorder ▲ | Redux |

Actions Settings

● ⚲ 🔒   Reset Revert Sweep Commit

filter...

@@INIT   4:55:28.07

multiply   +59:07.82

multiply   +58:20.11

Diff

Tree Raw

(pin): 10 => 100

(F12 Developer's Tools Interface)

2. React Redux

React Redux is the official React UI bindings layer for Redux. It lets your React components read data from a Redux store, and dispatch actions to the store to update the state. It implements many performance optimizations internally so that your own component only re-renders when it needs to.

There are two ways by which React-Redux connects a component to a redux store: 1) connect() or ... 2) hooks.

The recommended way to start new apps with React and Redux is by using the official template for Create React App, which takes advantage of Redux Toolkit and React Redux's integration with React components.

```
# Redux + Plain JS template
npx create-react-app my-app --template redux

# Redux + TypeScript template
npx create-react-app my-app --template redux-typescript
```

Alternatively, you can manually install Redux and Redux Toolkit, along with the React binding:

```
npm install redux @reduxjs/toolkit react-redux
npm install --save-dev @redux-devtools/core
```

2.1. Provider

Typically rendered at the top level, the <Provider> component makes the Redux store accessible to any nested components.

In addition to 'store', you may provide a context instance. If you do so, you will need to provide the same context instance to all of your connected components as well.

```
import React from 'react'
import ReactDOM from 'react-dom'
import { Provider } from 'react-redux'

import { App } from './App'
import createStore from './createReduxStore'

const store = createStore()

ReactDOM.render(
  <Provider store={store}>
    <App />
  </Provider>,
  document.getElementById('root')
)
```

Be aware of the difference between the following two statements:

```
import x from 'y';
```
```
import {x} from 'y';
```

2.2. connect

The connect() function connects a React component to a Redux store. It accepts four parameters, all optional:

1. **mapStateToProps?: (state, ownProps?) => stateProps**: This will be called anytime the store is updated. 'stateProps' must be a plain object. It will merge with the wrapped component's props. 'ownProps', if given, will cause the function to be called as well when the props of the wrapper component change. It will contain the wrapper component's props.

	(state) => stateProps	(state, ownProps) => stateProps
mapStateToProps runs when:	store state changes	store state changes or any field of ownProps is different
component re-renders when:	any field of stateProps is different	any field of stateProps is different or any field of ownProps is different

2. **mapDispatchToProps?: dispatchProps | (dispatch, ownProps?) => dispatchProps:**: This defines the action-dispatching functions that will be passed to the component's props. If this parameter is null or undefined, the component will receive props.dispatch() by default. Supplying this parameter, for instance, allows actions to be dispatched with props.increment() directly rather than props.dispatch(increment()). mapDispatchToProps can be defined as an object in the form {increment, decrement, ...}, or as a function returning {increment: ()=>dispatch(increment()), ...}. The second/functional form is more flexible as it has access to both dispatch() and ownProps. To bind multiple action creators at once, use the function bindActionCreators() from the 'redux' library: function mapDispatchToProps(dispatch) { return bindActionCreators({ increment, decrement, reset }, dispatch); }

3. **mergeProps?: (stateProps, dispatchProps, ownProps) => Object**: This defines the final props of the component. If undefined, the component will receive { ...stateProps, ...dispatchProps, ...ownProps } as its props.

4. **options?: Object**:
   i. **context?: Object:** This sets the context provided to <Provider>.
   ii. **pure?: boolean:** True by default, this indicates whether the component is 'pure' and does not rely on any input or state other than its props and the selected Redux store's state. When options.pure is true, connect() performs several equality checks (the next four functions) that are used to avoid unnecessary calls to mapStateToProps, mapDispatchToProps, mergeProps, and

ultimately to render. While the defaults are probably appropriate most of the times, you may wish to customize them.

iii. **areStatesEqual?: Function:** default value: strictEqual: (next, prev) => prev === next

iv. **areOwnPropsEqual?: Function:** default value: shallowEqual

v. **areStatePropsEqual?: Function:** default value: shallowEqual

vi. **areMergedPropsEqual?: Function:** default value: shallowEqual

vii. **forwardRef?: boolean:** If {forwardRef : true} has been passed to connect, adding a ref to the connected wrapper component will actually return the instance of the wrapped component.

Sample usage:

```
connect()(MyComponent)
connect(mapState)(MyComponent)
connect(mapState, null, mergeProps, options)(MyComponent)
```

As the store state changes, mapStateToProps() is invoked and the component is re-rendered.

```
// src/index.js
import React from "react";
import { createRoot } from "react-dom/client";
import { createStore } from "redux";
import { Provider } from "react-redux";
import reducer from "./reducer";
import App from "./App";

const store = createStore(reducer, 0);

const root = createRoot(document.getElementById("root"));

root.render(
  <Provider store={store}>
    <App />
  </Provider>
);
```

```
// src/reducer.js
export default function (state, action) {   // a reducer
  if (typeof state === "undefined") return 0;
  switch (action.type) {
    case "INCREMENT":
      return state + 1;
    case "DECREMENT":
      return state - 1;
    default:
      return state;
  }
}
```

```
// src/App.js

import { connect } from "react-redux";

const App = ({ v, increment }) => {
  return (
    <div>
      <span>{v}</span>
      <button onClick={increment}>+</button>
    </div>
  );
};
```

```
const mapStateToProps = (state) => {
  console.log("mapStateToProps() invoked");
  return { v: state };
};

const mapDispatchToProps = (dispatch) => ({
  increment: () => dispatch({ type: "INCREMENT" })
});

export default connect(mapStateToProps, mapDispatchToProps)(App);
```

0 [+]

https://codesandbox.io/s/react-redux-connect-kt9wlf

Notice the difference when including 'ownProps'. Below bindActionCreators() is used to combine action creators.

```
// src/index.js
import { createRoot } from "react-dom/client";
import { createStore } from "redux";
import { Provider } from "react-redux";
import reducer from "./reducer";
import App from "./App";

const store = createStore(reducer, 0);

const root = createRoot(document.getElementById("root"));

root.render(
  <Provider store={store}>
    <App />
  </Provider>
);
```

```
// src/reducer.js
export default function (state, action) {   // a reducer
  if (typeof state === "undefined") return 0;
  switch (action.type) {
    case "INCREMENT":
      return parseInt(state) + parseInt(action.s);
    case "DECREMENT":
      return parseInt(state) - parseInt(action.s);
    case "RESET":
      return 0;
    default:
      return state;
  }
}
```

```
// src/App.js
import { useState, useRef } from "react";
import { connect } from "react-redux";
import { bindActionCreators } from "redux";

const increment = (s) => ({ type: "INCREMENT", s }); // action creator
const decrement = (s) => ({ type: "DECREMENT", s }); // action creator

const mapStateToProps = (state, ownProps) => {
  // if ownProps is not supplied, this function won't be called
  // as the step prop changes
  console.log("mapStateToProps() invoked", state, ownProps);
  return { v: state };
```

12

```
};

const mapDispatchToProps = (dispatch, ownProps) => {
  // if ownProps is not supplied, this function won't be called
  // as the step prop changes
  console.log("mapDispatchToProps() invoked", ownProps);
  return {
    dispatch, // passing the generic dispatch() function too
    ...bindActionCreators({ increment, decrement, dispatch }, dispatch)
  };
};

const Counter = connect(
  mapStateToProps,
  mapDispatchToProps
)(({ v, increment, decrement, dispatch, step }) => {
  console.log(step);
  return (
    <div>
      <button onClick={() => decrement(step)}>-</button>
      value:<span>{v}</span>
      <button onClick={() => increment(step)}>+</button>
      <button onClick={() => dispatch({ type: "RESET" })}>RESET</button>
    </div>
  );
});

const App = () => {
  const stepInput = useRef(1);
  const [step, updateStep] = useState(1);
  return (
    <div>
      step:
      <input
        ref={stepInput}
        type="number"
        onChange={() => updateStep(stepInput.current.value)}/>
      <Counter step={step} />
    </div>
  );
};

export default App;
```

step: [   ]

[-] value:0 [+] | RESET

https://codesandbox.io/s/redux-react-connect-with-ownprops-5ms09b

13

If you ever pass 'context' to <Provider>, you will need to pass it every time you use connect(). Below we also compare if 'mergedProps' are equal and should thus avoid rerendering.

```
// src/index.js
import React from "react";
import { createRoot } from "react-dom/client";
import { createStore } from "redux";
import { Provider } from "react-redux";
import reducer from "./reducer";
import context from "./context";
import App from "./App";

const store = createStore(reducer, 0);
const myContext = context;
const root = createRoot(document.getElementById("root"));

root.render(
  <Provider store={store} context={myContext}>
    <App />
  </Provider>
);
```

```
// src/reducer.js
export default function (state, action) {   // a reducer
  if (typeof state === "undefined") return 0;
  switch (action.type) {
    case "INCREMENT":
      return parseInt(state) + parseInt(action.s);
    case "DECREMENT":
      return parseInt(state) - parseInt(action.s);
    case "RESET":
      return 0;
    default:
      return state;
  }
}
```

```
// src/context.js
import React from "react";
export default React.createContext();
```

```
// src/App.js
import React, { useState, useRef, useContext } from "react";
import { connect } from "react-redux";
import { bindActionCreators } from "redux";
import context from "./context";

const increment = (s) => ({ type: "INCREMENT", s }); // action creator
const decrement = (s) => ({ type: "DECREMENT", s }); // action creator

const mapStateToProps = (state) => {
  console.log("mapStateToProps() invoked", state);
  return { v: state };
};

const mapDispatchToProps = { increment, decrement }; // object form

const mergeProps = (stateProps, dispatchProps, ownProps) => {   // always called
  console.log("mergeProps() invoked");
  return {
    value: stateProps.v,
    plus: dispatchProps.increment,
    minus: dispatchProps.decrement,
    step: ownProps.step
  };
};
```

```jsx
const areMergedPropsEqual = (next, prev) => {   // always called
  console.log("areMergePropsEqual() invoked", prev, next);
  return prev === next || Math.abs(prev.value) > 10;
  // stop rerendering when value reaches 10
};

const Counter = connect(mapStateToProps, mapDispatchToProps, mergeProps, {
  context,
  areMergedPropsEqual
})((props) => {
  return (
    <context.Provider value={props}>
      <A />
    </context.Provider>
  );
});

const A = (props) => {
  return <B />;
};

const B = (props) => {
  return <C />;
};

const C = (props) => {
  const { step, value, plus, minus } = useContext(context);
  return (
    <div>
      <button onClick={() => minus(step)}>-</button>
      value:<span>{value}</span>
      <button onClick={() => plus(step)}>+</button>
    </div>
  );
};

const App = () => {
  const stepInput = useRef(1);
  const [step, updateStep] = useState(1);
  return (
    <div>
      step:
      <input
        ref={stepInput}
        type="number"
        onChange={() => updateStep(stepInput.current.value)} />
      <Counter step={step} />
    </div>
  );
};

export default App;
```

step: [_____]

[-] value:0 [+]

https://codesandbox.io/s/react-redux-connect-with-context-mergedprops-and-aremergedpropsequal-lnwryh

2.3. useSelector & useDispatch

useSelector() allows you to access the state of your Redux store.

useDispatch() returns a copy of the dispatch() function of the Redux store.

As the store state changes, the component is re-rendered. Dispatching an action causes useSelector() to be called.

```
// src/index.js
import React from "react";
import { createRoot } from "react-dom/client";
import { createStore } from "redux";
import { Provider } from "react-redux";
import reducer from "./reducer";
import App from "./App";

const store = createStore(reducer, 0);

const root = createRoot(document.getElementById("root"));

root.render(
  <Provider store={store}>
    <App />
  </Provider>
);
```

```
// src/reducer.js
export default function (state, action) {   // a reducer
  if (typeof state === "undefined") return 0;
  switch (action.type) {
    case "INCREMENT":
      return state + 1;
    case "DECREMENT":
      return state - 1;
    default:
      return state;
  }
}
```

```
// src/App.js
import { useSelector, useDispatch } from "react-redux";

export default () => {
  console.log("rendering...");
  const v = useSelector((state) => {
    console.log("useSelector() invoked");
    return state;
  });

  const dispatch = useDispatch();

  return (
    <div>
      <span>{v}</span>
      <button onClick={() => dispatch({ type: "INCREMENT" })}>+</button>
    </div>
  );
};
```

```
0  +
```

https://codesandbox.io/s/react-redux-hooks-9kgpbk

16

Every time an action is dispatched, useSelector() only forces a re-render if the selector result appears to be different than the last result. You can define your own equality function too: (next, prev)=>Boolean.

```js
// src/index.js
import React from "react";
import { createRoot } from "react-dom/client";
import { createStore } from "redux";
import { Provider } from "react-redux";
import reducer from "./reducer";
import App from "./App";

const store = createStore(reducer, 0);

const root = createRoot(document.getElementById("root"));

root.render(
  <Provider store={store}>
    <App />
  </Provider>
);
```

```js
// src/reducer.js
export default function (state, action) {  // a reducer
  if (typeof state === "undefined") return 0;
  switch (action.type) {
    case "INCREMENT":
      return state + 1;
    case "DECREMENT":
      return state - 1;
    case "RESET":
      return 0;
    default:
      return state;
  }
}
```

```js
// src/App.js
import { useSelector, useDispatch, shallowEqual } from "react-redux";

export default () => {
  console.log("rendering...");
  const store = useSelector((state) => {
    console.log("useSelector() invoked", { v: state });
    return { v: 0 };
  }, shallowEqual);
  const dispatch = useDispatch();
  return (
    <div>
      <span>{store.v}</span>
      <button onClick={() => dispatch({ type: "INCREMENT" })}>+</button>
    </div>
  );
};
```

0 +

https://codesandbox.io/s/react-redux-hooks-shallowequal-r354zh

Without useCallback(), 'increment' would point to a different memory reference every time the wrapper component is rendered, thus triggering the re-rendering of <Plus>.

```js
// src/index.js
import React from "react";
import { createRoot } from "react-dom/client";
import { createStore } from "redux";
import { Provider } from "react-redux";
import reducer from "./reducer";
import App from "./App";

const store = createStore(reducer, 0);

const root = createRoot(document.getElementById("root"));

root.render(
  <Provider store={store}>
    <App />
  </Provider>
);
```

```js
// src/reducer.js
export default function (state, action) {   // a reducer
  if (typeof state === "undefined") return 0;
  switch (action.type) {
    case "INCREMENT":
      return state + 1;
    case "DECREMENT":
      return state - 1;
    case "RESET":
      return 0;
    default:
      return state;
  }
}
```

```js
// src/App.js
import { useCallback, memo } from "react";
import { useSelector, useDispatch } from "react-redux";

const Plus = memo(({ onIncrement }) => {
  console.log("rendering <Plus>...");
  return <button onClick={onIncrement}>+</button>;
});

export default () => {
  console.log("rendering <App>...");
  const v = useSelector((state) => {
    console.log("useSelector() invoked");
    return state;
  });
  const dispatch = useDispatch();
  const increment = useCallback(() => dispatch({ type: "INCREMENT" }), [dispatch]);
  return (
    <div>
      <span>{v}</span>
      <Plus onIncrement={increment} />
    </div>
  );
};
```

0 +

https://codesandbox.io/s/react-redux-hooks-memoization-x0ryc0

18

2.4. useStore

useStore() returns a copy of the Redux store passed to <Provider>.

This may be useful for less common scenarios requiring access to the store, such as replacing reducers.

Below, dispatching an action will not trigger a re-render of the component. In general, you should use useSelector() and useDispatch() instead.

```
// src/index.js
import React from "react";
import { createRoot } from "react-dom/client";
import { createStore } from "redux";
import { Provider } from "react-redux";
import reducer from "./reducer";
import App from "./App";

const store = createStore(reducer, 0);

const root = createRoot(document.getElementById("root"));

store.subscribe(() => console.log(store.getState()));

root.render(
  <Provider store={store}>
    <App />
  </Provider>
);
```

```
// src/reducer.js
export default function (state, action) {    // a reducer
  if (typeof state === "undefined") return 0;
  switch (action.type) {
    case "INCREMENT":
      return state + 1;
    case "DECREMENT":
      return state - 1;
    default:
      return state;
  }
}
```

```
// src/App.js
import { useStore } from "react-redux";
export default () => {
  console.log("rendering...");
  const store = useStore();
  return (
    <div>
      <span>{store.getState()}</span>
      <button onClick={() => store.dispatch({ type: "INCREMENT" })}>+</button>
    </div>
  );
};
```

0 [+]

https://codesandbox.io/s/react-redux-hooks-usestore-6z3zu6

19

2.5. Custom Hooks

Recipe 1: useActions()

```
// src/index.js
import React from "react";
import { createRoot } from "react-dom/client";
import { createStore } from "redux";
import { Provider } from "react-redux";
import reducer from "./reducer";
import App from "./App";

const store = createStore(reducer, 0);

const root = createRoot(document.getElementById("root"));

store.subscribe(() => console.log(store.getState()));

root.render(
  <Provider store={store}>
    <App />
  </Provider>
);
```

```
// src/reducer.js
export default function (state, action) {   // a reducer
  if (typeof state === "undefined") return 0;
  switch (action.type) {
    case "INCREMENT":
      return state + 1;
    case "DECREMENT":
      return state - 1;
    default:
      return state;
  }
}
```

```
// src/actions.js
export const increment = () => ({ type: "INCREMENT" });
export const decrement = () => ({ type: "DECREMENT" });
```

```
// src/hooks.js
import { bindActionCreators } from "redux";
import { useDispatch } from "react-redux";
import { useMemo } from "react";

export function useActions(actions, deps) {
  const dispatch = useDispatch();
  return useMemo(
    () => {
      if (Array.isArray(actions)) {
        return actions.map((a) => bindActionCreators(a, dispatch));
      }
      return bindActionCreators(actions, dispatch);
    },
    deps ? [dispatch, ...deps] : [dispatch]);
}
```

```
// src/App.js
import { useSelector } from "react-redux";
import { useActions } from "./hooks";
import { increment, decrement } from "./actions";

export default () => {
  const v = useSelector((state) => state);
  const a = useActions({ increment, decrement }, []);
```

```
    return (
      <div>
        <button onClick={a.decrement}>-</button>
        <span>{v}</span>
        <button onClick={a.increment}>+</button>
      </div>
    );
};
```

| - | 0 | + |

https://codesandbox.io/s/react-redux-hooks-useactions-k59j1r

Recipe 2: useShallowEqualSelector()

Here, if useSelector() were used instead of useShallowEqualSelector(), repeated clicks on the RESET button would trigger re-rendering of the component as the state {value:0}!=={value:0}, ie. different memory reference.

```
// src/index.js
import React from "react";
import { createRoot } from "react-dom/client";
import { createStore } from "redux";
import { Provider } from "react-redux";
import reducer from "./reducer";
import App from "./App";

const store = createStore(reducer, { value: 0 });
const root = createRoot(document.getElementById("root"));
store.subscribe(() => console.log(store.getState()));
root.render(
  <Provider store={store}>
    <App />
  </Provider>
);
```

```
// src/reducer.js
export default function (state, action) {   // a reducer
  if (typeof state === "undefined") return 0;
  switch (action.type) {
    case "INCREMENT":
      return { value: state.value + 1 };
    case "DECREMENT":
      return { value: state.value - 1 };
    case "RESET":
      return { value: 0 };
    default:
      return { value: state.value };
  }
}
```

```
// src/actions.js
export const increment = () => ({ type: "INCREMENT" });
export const decrement = () => ({ type: "DECREMENT" });
```

```
// src/hooks.js
import { useSelector, shallowEqual } from "react-redux";
export function useShallowEqualSelector(selector) {
  return useSelector(selector, shallowEqual);
}
```

```
// src/App.js
import { useDispatch, useSelector } from "react-redux";
import { useShallowEqualSelector } from "./hooks";
export default () => {
  console.log("rendering component...");
  const v = useShallowEqualSelector((state) => state).value;
  const dispatch = useDispatch();
  return (
    <div>
      <button onClick={() => dispatch({ type: "DECREMENT" })}>-</button>
      <span>{v}</span>
      <button onClick={() => dispatch({ type: "INCREMENT" })}>+</button>
      <button onClick={() => dispatch({ type: "RESET" })}>RESET</button>
    </div>
  );
};
```

| - | 0 | + | RESET |

https://codesandbox.io/s/react-redux-hooks-useshallowequalselector-2dp5c4

22

3. Redux Toolkit

So far, we have been coding Redux applications in a legacy way.

The recommended way to write Redux applications is to use Redux Toolkit, a library built on top of Redux that speeds up development and makes your code more maintainable.

3.1. configureStore

Building on createStore(), configureStore():

- accepts a readable named options object, with the keys 'preloadedState', 'reducer', 'middleware', 'enhancers', and 'devTools'.
- accepts arrays of middleware and enhancers by calling applyMiddleware() and compose() automatically.
- can call combineReducers() automatically.
- enables Redux DevTools Extension automatically by default.
- adds the 'redux-thunk' middleware automatically.
- adds middleware that checks for common mistakes like mutating the state or using non-serializable values in development.

...no more applyMiddleware() and compose()!

```
// src/index.js
import React from "react";
import { createRoot } from "react-dom/client";
import { Provider } from "react-redux";
import store from "./store";
import App from "./App";

const root = createRoot(document.getElementById("root"));

root.render(
  <Provider store={store}>
    <App />
  </Provider>
);
```

```
// src/reducer.js
export default function (state, action) {    // a reducer
  if (typeof state === "undefined") return 0;
  switch (action.type) {
    case "INCREMENT":
      return state + 1;
    case "DECREMENT":
      return state - 1;
    default:
      return state;
  }
}
```

```
// src/store.js
import reducer from "./reducer";
import { configureStore } from "@reduxjs/toolkit";

const alerter = ({ getState }) => (next) => (action) => {
  alert(getState() + " ...before");
  next(action);
  return action;
```

```
};
const logger = ({ getState }) => (next) => (action) => {
  console.log(getState() + " ...before");
  next(action);
  return action;
};

export default configureStore({
  reducer, // ES6, ie.: reducer:reducer
  preloadedState: 100,
  middleware: [alerter, logger],
  enhancers: [],
  devTools: process.env.NODE_ENV !== "production"
});
```

```
// src/App.js
import { useSelector, useDispatch } from "react-redux";

export default () => {
  console.log("rendering...");
  const v = useSelector((state) => {
    console.log("useSelector() invoked");
    return state;
  });
  const dispatch = useDispatch();
  return (
    <div>
      <span>{v}</span>
      <button onClick={() => dispatch({ type: "INCREMENT" })}>+</button>
    </div>
  );
};
```

```
100 +
```

https://codesandbox.io/s/redux-toolkit-configurestore-mizjob

The default middleware is not included if you explicitly state a value for the
'middleware' key. Assign a callback accepting a defaultMiddleware argument if
you want to add to the default middleware.

```
// src/index.js
import React from "react";
import { createRoot } from "react-dom/client";
import { Provider } from "react-redux";
import store from "./store";
import App from "./App";

const root = createRoot(document.getElementById("root"));

root.render(
  <Provider store={store}>
    <App />
  </Provider>
);
```

```
// src/reducer.js
export default function (state, action) {    // a reducer
  if (typeof state === "undefined") return 0;
  switch (action.type) {
    case "INCREMENT":
      return state + 1;
    case "DECREMENT":
```

```
          return state - 1;
       default:
          return state;
    }
}
```

```
// src/store.js
import reducer from "./reducer";
import { configureStore } from "@reduxjs/toolkit";

const alerter = ({ getState }) => (next) => (action) => {
  alert(getState() + " ...before");
  next(action);
  return action;
};

const logger = ({ getState }) => (next) => (action) => {
  console.log(getState() + " ...before");
  next(action);
  return action;
};

export default configureStore({
  reducer, // ES6, ie.: reducer:reducer
  preloadedState: 100,
  middleware: (defaultMiddleware) => defaultMiddleware().concat([alerter, logger]),
  enhancers: []
});
```

```
// src/App.js
import { useSelector, useDispatch } from "react-redux";

export default () => {
  console.log("rendering...");
  const v = useSelector((state) => {
    console.log("useSelector() invoked");
    return state;
  });
  const dispatch = useDispatch();

  return (
    <div>
      <span>{v}</span>
      <button onClick={() => dispatch({ type: "INCREMENT" })}>+</button>
    </div>
  );
};
```

100 [+]

https://codesandbox.io/s/
redux-toolkit-configurestore-adding-to-default-middleware-c2zh3h

...no more combineReducers()!
If you want to nest reducers to more than one levels, you'll still need to call
combineReducers().

```
// src/index.js
import React from "react";
import { createRoot } from "react-dom/client";
import { Provider } from "react-redux";
import store from "./store";
import App from "./App";
```

```
const root = createRoot(document.getElementById("root"));

root.render(
  <Provider store={store}>
    <App />
  </Provider>
);
```

```
// src/reducers.js
export function counter(state = 0, action) {    // a reducer
  if (typeof state === "undefined") return 0;
  switch (action.type) {
    case "INCREMENT":  return state + 1;
    case "DECREMENT": return state - 1;
    default:              return state;
  }
}
export function mfunc(state = 2, action) {    // another reducer
  switch (action.type) {
    case "POW": return state ** action.n;
    case "MUL": return state * action.n;
    default:      return state;
  }
}
```

```
// src/store.js
import { counter, mfunc } from "./reducers";
import { configureStore } from "@reduxjs/toolkit";

export default configureStore({
  reducer: {
    x: counter,
    y: mfunc
  }
});
```

```
// src/App.js
import { useSelector, useDispatch } from "react-redux";

export default () => {
  console.log("rendering...");
  const s = useSelector((state) => {
    console.log("useSelector() invoked");
    return state;
  });
  const dispatch = useDispatch();
  return (
    <div>
      <button onClick={() => dispatch({ type: "INCREMENT" })}>+1</button>
      <span>{s.x}</span>
      <br />
      <button onClick={() => dispatch({ type: "MUL", n: 3 })}>*3</button>
      <span>{s.y}</span>
    </div>
  );
};
```

+1 | 0
*3 | 2

26

enhancers: [offline] will result in a final setup of [applyMiddleware, offline, devToolsExtension].

enhancers: (defaultEnhancers) => [offline, ...defaultEnhancers] will result in a final setup of [offline, applyMiddleware, devToolsExtension].

3.2. configureStore ... Middleware

In **development mode**, the default middleware is:

- Immutability check middleware: deeply compares state values for mutations. It can detect mutations in reducers during a dispatch, and also mutations that occur between dispatches (such as in a component or a selector). When a mutation is detected, it will throw an error and indicate the key path for where the mutated value was detected in the state tree. (Forked from redux-immutable-state-invariant.)
- Serializability check middleware: Deeply checks your state tree and your actions for non-serializable values such as functions, Promises, Symbols, and other non-plain-JS-data values. When a non-serializable value is detected, a console error will be printed with the key path for where the non-serializable value was detected.
- redux-thunk

ie.:

```
const middleware = [thunk, immutableStateInvariant, serializableStateInvariant]
```

Note that by right, you are supposed to return a new instance of your state in your reducers. You are NOT supposed to mutate the state object in place in your reducers or through a reference of the state.

In **product mode**, the default middleware is:

- redux-thunk

ie.:

```
const middleware = [thunk]
```

Each piece of the middleware can be configured in getDefaultMiddleware(), by either passing 'false' to get excluded, or passing the matching options object for its corresponding field.

```
const store = configureStore({
  reducer: rootReducer,
  middleware: (getDefaultMiddleware) =>
    getDefaultMiddleware({
      immutableCheck: {
        ignoredPaths: ['ignoredPath', 'ignoredNested.one', 'ignoredNested.two'],
      },
      serializableCheck: false,
      thunk: {
        extraArgument: myCustomApiService,
      }
    }),
})
```

createImmutableStateInvariantMiddleware() allows you to specify which state paths to skip checking for mutations.

```
import { createSlice } from '@reduxjs/toolkit'
export const exampleSlice = createSlice({
  name: 'example',
  initialState: {
    user: 'will track changes',
    ignoredPath: 'single level',
    ignoredNested: {
      a: 'one',
      b: 'two',
    },
  },
  reducers: {},
});
export default exampleSlice.reducer;
```

```
import { configureStore, createImmutableStateInvariantMiddleware}
                                            from '@reduxjs/toolkit';
import exampleSliceReducer from './exampleSlice';
const immutableInvariantMiddleware = createImmutableStateInvariantMiddleware({
  ignoredPaths: ['ignoredPath', 'ignoredNested.a', 'ignoredNested.b'],
  warnAfter?: 100,     // prints a warning if checks take longer than 100ms
  isImmutable?: IsImmutableFunc   // Callback function to check if a value is considered to be
                                  // immutable. Applied recursively to every value in the state.
                                  // 'true' for primitive types.
})
const store = configureStore({
  reducer: exampleSliceReducer,
  middleware: [immutableInvariantMiddleware],     // replacing all default middleware
})
```

createSerializableStateInvariantMiddleware() detects if any non-serializable values have been included in the state or dispatched actions.

```
import { Iterable } from 'immutable'
import {
  configureStore,
  createSerializableStateInvariantMiddleware,
  isPlain,
} from '@reduxjs/toolkit'
import reducer from './reducer';
const isSerializable = (value) => Iterable.isIterable(value) || isPlain(value);
const getEntries = (value) => Iterable.isIterable(value) ? value.entries() : Object.entries(value);
const serializableMiddleware = createSerializableStateInvariantMiddleware({
  isSerializable,        // The function to check if a value is considered serializable. This function is
                         // applied recursively to every value contained in the state. Defaults to
                         // `isPlain()`.
  getEntries,            // The function that will be used to retrieve entries from each value. If
                         // unspecified, `Object.entries` will be used. Defaults to `undefined`.
  // ignoredActions,     // An array of action types (strings) to ignore when checking for
                         // serializability. Defaults to [].
  // ignoredActionPaths, // An array of dot-separated path strings to ignore when checking for
                         // serializability, Defaults to ['meta.arg', 'meta.baseQueryMeta'].
  // ignoredPaths,       // An array of dot-separated path strings to ignore when checking for
                         //serializability, Defaults to [].
  warnAfter: 100,        // Warns if checking takes longer than 100ms. Defaults to 32.
  // ignoreState: true,  // Opt out of checking state. When set to `true`, other state-related
                         // params will be ignored.
  // ignoreActions: true // Opt out of checking actions. When set to `true`, other action-related
                         // params will be ignored.
});
const store = configureStore({reducer, middleware: [serializableMiddleware]}));
```

3.3. configureStore ... Listener Middleware

You can define 'listener' entries that are fired in response to Redux store updates.

In contrast to listeners specified by store.subscribe() which are fired on all dispatch actions, listeners supplied to listenerMiddleware.startListening() are fired on certain actions only.

Use one of the four ways to specify when a listener will be fired -- 'type', 'actionCreator', 'matcher', or 'predicate'. Notice when the listeners are fired relative to the updates and rendering.

/src/index.js
```
import React from "react";
import { createRoot } from "react-dom/client";
import { Provider } from "react-redux";
import store from "./store";
import App from "./App";

const root = createRoot(document.getElementById("root"));
store.subscribe(() => console.log("invoking listeners..."));
root.render(
  <Provider store={store}>
    <App />
  </Provider>
);
```

/src/reducer.js
```
export default function (state, action) {
  // a reducer
  if (typeof state === "undefined") return 0;
  console.log("updating...");
  switch (action.type) {
    case "INCREMENT":
      return state + 1;
    case "DECREMENT":
      return state - 1;
    default:
      return state;
  }
}
```

/src/store.js
```
import reducer from "./reducer";
import {
  configureStore,
  createListenerMiddleware,
  createAction,
  isAnyOf
} from "@reduxjs/toolkit";

let increment = createAction("INCREMENT");
let decrement = createAction("DECREMENT");

const listenerMiddleware = createListenerMiddleware({
  extra: {
    // optional
    x: 100 // to be passed to listenerApi (see explanation below)
  },
  onError: (error, errorInfo) => {
    // optional
    console.log(error);
    console.log("raised by: " + errorInfo.raisedBy); // 'effect' or 'predicate'
  }
});
```

```
listenerMiddleware.startListening({
  type: "DECREMENT", // notation 1
  effect: async (action, listenerApi) => console.log("Listener 1: DECREMENT")
});
listenerMiddleware.startListening({
  actionCreator: increment, // notation 2
  effect: async (action, listenerApi) => console.log("Listener 2: INCREMENT")
});
listenerMiddleware.clearListeners(); // removes listeners 1 and 2
const listener = {
  matcher: isAnyOf(increment, decrement), // notation 3
  effect: async (action, listenerApi) => {
    await listenerApi.delay(3000); // pausing for possible cancellation
    console.log("Listener 3: INCREMENT or DECREMENT");
  }
};
const unsubscribe = listenerMiddleware.startListening(listener);
export { unsubscribe };
listenerMiddleware.startListening(listener); // repeated listener not added
//listenerMiddleware.stopListening(listener);   // removes listener 3

listenerMiddleware.startListening({
  predicate: (action, currentState, previousState) => {  // notation 4
    console.log("Listener 4: " + JSON.stringify(action));   // eg. {type: "INCREMENT"}
    //throw 'my error';
    return previousState === 100; // fires when true
  },
  effect: async (action, listenerApi) => console.log("from 100")
});

export default configureStore({
  reducer, // ES6, ie.:  reducer:reducer
  preloadedState: 100,
  middleware: (getDefaultMiddleware) =>
    getDefaultMiddleware().prepend(listenerMiddleware.middleware)
});
```

/src/App.js
```
import { useSelector, useDispatch } from "react-redux";
import { unsubscribe } from "./store";
export default () => {
  const v = useSelector((state) => state);
  const dispatch = useDispatch();
  console.log("rendering " + v + " ...");
  return (
    <div>
      <button onClick={() => dispatch({ type: "DECREMENT" })}>-</button>
      <span>{v}</span>
      <button onClick={() => dispatch({ type: "INCREMENT" })}>+</button>
      <button onClick={() => unsubscribe({ cancelActive: true })}>
        cancel and unsubscribe
      </button>
    </div>
  );
};
```

| - | 100 | + | cancel and unsubscribe |

https://codesandbox.io/s/
redux-toolkit-configurestore-listener-middleware-gouxv6

You can dynamically add and remove listeners at runtime by dispatching special "add" and "remove" actions.

To do so, first import addListener(), removeListener(), clearAllListeners() from "@reduxjs/toolkit".

```
const unsubscribe = store.dispatch(addListener({ predicate, effect }));
                         // same arguments as startListening() above const wasRemoved
= store.dispatch(removeListener({ predicate, effect, cancelActive: true }));
                         // same arguments as stopListening() above
store.dispatch(clearAllListeners());
```

listenerApi, the second argument of the effect callback, has the following members:

Store Interaction
- dispatch(): the standard store.dispatch() method.
- getState(): the standard store.getState() method.
- getOriginalState(): the state before the reducers ran.
- extra: the object passed to the 'extra' property of createListenerMiddleware().
-

Subscription Management
- unsubscribe(): prevents the listener from running in future.
- subscribe(): re-subscribes the listener if it was previously unsubscribed.
- cancelActiveListeners(): cancels all other running instances of this same listener except for the one that made this call.
- signal: An AbortSignal object whose 'aborted' property will be set to true if the listener execution is aborted or completed.

'Cancellable' Conditional Workflow
- take(predicate, timeoutMs): waits for another dispatch action and returns a promise that will resolve to (action, currentState, previousState) when the predicate returns true. If a timeout is provided and expires first, the promise resolves to null.
- condition(predicate, timeoutMs): waits for another dispatch action and returns a promise that will resolve to true if the predicate succeeds, and false if a timeout is provided and expires first.
- delay(timeoutMs): returns a promise that resolves after the timeout, or rejects if cancelled before the expiration.
- pause(promise): accepts any promise, and returns a promise that either resolves with the argument promise or rejects if canceled before the resolution.

Child Forking
- fork(forkApi): launches a child task asynchronously.

As you use the listenerApi functions 'condition', 'take', 'pause', and 'delay', you may cancel the listener when it is running, with unsubscribe({ cancelActive: true }) for instance.

/src/index.js
```
import React from "react";
import { createRoot } from "react-dom/client";
import { Provider } from "react-redux";
import store from "./store";
import App from "./App";

const root = createRoot(document.getElementById("root"));
root.render(
  <Provider store={store}>
    <App />
  </Provider>
);
```

/src/reducer.js
```
export default function (state, action) {
  // a reducer
  if (typeof state === "undefined") return 0;
  switch (action.type) {
    case "INCREMENT":
      return state + 1;
    case "DECREMENT":
      return state - 1;
    default:
      return state;
  }
}
```

/src/store.js
```
import reducer from "./reducer";
import {
  configureStore,
  createListenerMiddleware,
  createAction,
  isAnyOf
} from "@reduxjs/toolkit";

let increment = createAction("INCREMENT");
let decrement = createAction("DECREMENT");

const listenerMiddleware = createListenerMiddleware();

const someTasks = (ms) => new Promise((resolve) => setTimeout(resolve, ms));
const isIncrement = (action, currentState, previousState) => {
  return action.type === "INCREMENT";
};
listenerMiddleware.startListening({
  matcher: isAnyOf(increment, decrement),
  effect: async (action, listenerApi) => {
    console.log("effect");
    if (await listenerApi.condition(isIncrement)) {
      console.log("is INCREMENT");
      await listenerApi.pause(someTasks(3000));
                              // identical to listenerApi.delay(3000) here
      console.log("paused for 3s");
      const r = await listenerApi.take(isIncrement, 2000);
      console.log(r);
    }
  }
});

export default configureStore({
```

```
  reducer, // ES6, ie.: reducer:reducer
  preloadedState: 0,
  middleware: (getDefaultMiddleware) =>
    getDefaultMiddleware().prepend(listenerMiddleware.middleware)
});
```

/src/App.js
```
import { useSelector, useDispatch } from "react-redux";

export default () => {
  const v = useSelector((state) => state);
  const dispatch = useDispatch();
  return (
    <div>
      <button onClick={() => dispatch({ type: "DECREMENT" })}>-</button>
      <span>{v}</span>
      <button onClick={() => dispatch({ type: "INCREMENT" })}>+</button>
    </div>
  );
};
```

```
 - |0| + 
```

https://codesandbox.io/s/
redux-toolkit-configurestore-listener-middleware-conditionals-bh5cyo

An example of this might be a listener that forks a child task containing an infinite loop that listens for events from a server. The parent then uses listenerApi.condition() to wait for a 'stop' action and cancels the child task.

/src/index.js
```
import React from "react";
import { createRoot } from "react-dom/client";
import { Provider } from "react-redux";
import store from "./store";
import App from "./App";

const root = createRoot(document.getElementById("root"));
root.render(
  <Provider store={store}>
    <App />
  </Provider>
);
```

/src/reducer.js
```
export default function (state, action) {
  if (typeof state === "undefined") return 0;
  switch (action.type) {
    case "INCREMENT":
      return state + 1;
    case "DECREMENT":
      return state - 1;
    default:
      return state;
  }
}
```

/src/store.js
```
import reducer from "./reducer";
import {
  configureStore,
  createListenerMiddleware,
  createAction,
  isAnyOf
} from "@reduxjs/toolkit";
```

34

```
let increment = createAction("INCREMENT");
let decrement = createAction("DECREMENT");

const listenerMiddleware = createListenerMiddleware();

const someTasks = (ms) => new Promise((resolve) => setTimeout(resolve, ms));

listenerMiddleware.startListening({
  matcher: isAnyOf(increment, decrement),
  effect: async (action, listenerApi) => {
    const task = listenerApi.fork(async (forkApi) => {
      console.log("performing some tasks");
      await forkApi.pause(someTasks(3000)); // identical to listenerApi.delay(3000)
      console.log("delaying 2s");
      await forkApi.delay(2000);
      console.log("forkApi.signal", forkApi.signal);
      return 42;
    });
    //task.cancel();
    console.log("waiting for child...");
    const result = await task.result;
    if (result.status === "ok") {
      console.log("Child succeeded: ", result.value);
    }
  }
});

export default configureStore({
  reducer, // ES6, ie.: reducer:reducer
  preloadedState: 0,
  middleware: (getDefaultMiddleware) =>
    getDefaultMiddleware().prepend(listenerMiddleware.middleware)
});
```

/src/App.js

```
import { useSelector, useDispatch } from "react-redux";

export default () => {
  const v = useSelector((state) => state);
  const dispatch = useDispatch();
  return (
    <div>
      <button onClick={() => dispatch({ type: "DECREMENT" })}>-</button>
      <span>{v}</span>
      <button onClick={() => dispatch({ type: "INCREMENT" })}>+</button>
    </div>
  );
};
```

```
- |0| +
```

https://codesandbox.io/s/
redux-toolkit-configurestore-listener-middleware-forking-89v7wh

It's best to create the listener middleware in a separate file (eg.
app/listenerMiddleware.js) rather than in the same file as the store. You can:

1. import effect callbacks from slice files into the middleware file, and add the listeners:

```
// app/listenerMiddleware.js
import { action1, listener1 } from '../features/feature1/feature1Slice'
import { action2, listener2 } from '../features/feature2/feature1Slice'
```

```
listenerMiddleware.startListening({ actionCreator: action1, effect: listener1 })
listenerMiddleware.startListening({ actionCreator: action2, effect: listener2 })
```

2. have the slice files import the middleware and directly add their listeners:

```
import { listenerMiddleware } from '../../app/listenerMiddleware'

const feature1Slice = createSlice(/* */)
const { action1 } = feature1Slice.actions

export default feature1Slice.reducer

listenerMiddleware.startListening({
  actionCreator: action1,
  effect: () => {},
})
```

3. create a setup function in the slice, but let the listener file call that on startup:

```
import type { AppStartListening } from '../../app/listenerMiddleware'

const feature1Slice = createSlice(/* */)
const { action1 } = feature1Slice.actions

export default feature1Slice.reducer

export const addFeature1Listeners = (startListening: AppStartListening) => {
  startListening({
    actionCreator: action1,
    effect: () => {},
  })
}
```

```
// app/listenerMiddleware.js
import { addFeature1Listeners } from '../features/feature1/feature1Slice'

addFeature1Listeners(listenerMiddleware.startListening)
```

3.4.   createAction & createReducer

Redux Toolkit provides a direct way to define an action creator, eg.:

```
const increment = createAction('counter/increment');
```

which is equivalent to:

```
function increment(amount) {
  return {
    type: 'counter/increment',
    payload: amount,
  }
}
```

createAction() accepts an optional second argument: a "prepare callback" that will be used to construct the payload value., eg.:

```
import { createAction, nanoid } from '@reduxjs/toolkit'
const addTodo = createAction('todos/add', function prepare(text) {
  return {
    payload: {
      text,
      id: nanoid(),
      createdAt: new Date().toISOString(),
    },
    meta: {
      x: 10
    },
    error: false
  }
})
console.log(addTodo('Write more docs'))
/*
  {
    type: 'todos/add',
    payload: {
      text: 'Write more docs',
      id: 'ruddl8iwbhf',
      createdAt: '2019-10-03T07:53:36.581Z'
    },
    meta: {
      x:10
    },
    error: false
  }
*/
```

An action creator returned from createAction() has the method match(), which can be called to test for equality:

```
const increment = createAction('INCREMENT')
function someFunction(action) {
  // accessing action.payload might result in an error here
  if (increment.match(action)) {
    // action.payload can be used here
  }
}
const chosen_actions = (actions) =>   // actions is an array of actions
  actions
    .filter(increment.match)
    .map((action) => {
      // action.payload can be safely here
    })
);
```

You can use one of the two createReducer() notations to easily define a reducer:

1. 'Builder Callback' notation

/src/index.js
```
import React from "react";
import { createRoot } from "react-dom/client";
import { Provider } from "react-redux";
import store from "./store";
import App from "./App";

const root = createRoot(document.getElementById("root"));
root.render(
  <Provider store={store}>
   <App />
  </Provider>
);
```

/src/reducer.js
```
import { createAction, createReducer } from "@reduxjs/toolkit";

const initialState = 0;
const plusAction = createAction("plus");
const minusAction = createAction("minus");

export { plusAction, minusAction };
export default createReducer(initialState, (builder) => {
 builder
   .addCase(minusAction, (state, action) => state - action.payload)
   .addCase(plusAction, (state, action) => state + action.payload)
   .addMatcher(
    // divide10, multiply10
    (action) => action.type.endsWith("10"),
    (state, action) => (action.type[0] === "d" ? state / 10 : state * 10)
   )
   .addDefaultCase(() => initialState); // reset
});
```

/src/store.js
```
import reducer from "./reducer";
import { configureStore } from "@reduxjs/toolkit";

export default configureStore({
 reducer, // ES6, ie.: reducer:reducer
 preloadedState: 10
});
```

/src/App.js
```
import { useSelector, useDispatch } from "react-redux";
import { plusAction, minusAction } from "./reducer";

export default () => {
 const v = useSelector((state) => state);
 const dispatch = useDispatch();
 return (
   <div>
    <button onClick={() => dispatch({ type: "divide10" })}>/10</button>
    <button onClick={() => dispatch(minusAction(10))}>-10</button>
    <button onClick={() => dispatch(minusAction(1))}>-1</button>
    <span>{v}</span>
    <button onClick={() => dispatch(plusAction(1))}>+1</button>
    <button onClick={() => dispatch({ type: "plus", payload: 10 })}>
     +10
    </button>
    <button onClick={() => dispatch({ type: "multiply10" })}>*10</button>
    <button onClick={() => dispatch({ type: "reset" })}>reset</button>
   </div>
 );
};
```

https://codesandbox.io/s/redux-toolkit-createaction-createreducer-xv5yz8

2. 'Map Object' notation (deprecated)

/src/index.js
```
import React from "react";
import { createRoot } from "react-dom/client";
import { Provider } from "react-redux";
import store from "./store";
import App from "./App";

const root = createRoot(document.getElementById("root"));
root.render(
  <Provider store={store}>
    <App />
  </Provider>
);
```

/src/reducer.js
```
import { createAction, createReducer } from "@reduxjs/toolkit";

const initialState = 0;
const plusAction = createAction("plus");
const minusAction = createAction("minus");

export { plusAction, minusAction };
export default createReducer(
  initialState,
  {
    // ...like addCase()
    minus: (state, action) => state - action.payload,
    [plusAction]: (state, action) => state + action.payload
  },
  [
    // ...like addMatcher()
    {
      matcher: (action) => action.type.endsWith("10"),
      reducer: (state, action) =>
        action.type[0] === "d" ? state / 10 : state * 10
    }
  ],
  () => initialState // ...like addDefaultCase()
);
```

/src/store.js
```
import reducer from "./reducer";
import { configureStore } from "@reduxjs/toolkit";

export default configureStore({
  reducer, // ES6, ie.:  reducer:reducer
  preloadedState: 10
});
```

/src/App.js
```
import { useSelector, useDispatch } from "react-redux";
import { plusAction, minusAction } from "./reducer";

export default () => {
  const v = useSelector((state) => state);
  const dispatch = useDispatch();
  return (
    <div>
      <button onClick={() => dispatch({ type: "divide10" })}>/10</button>
      <button onClick={() => dispatch(minusAction(10))}>-10</button>
```

```
      <button onClick={() => dispatch(minusAction(1))}>-1</button>
      <span>{v}</span>
      <button onClick={() => dispatch(plusAction(1))}>+1</button>
      <button onClick={() => dispatch({ type: "plus", payload: 10 })}>
        +10
      </button>
      <button onClick={() => dispatch({ type: "multiply10" })}>*10</button>
      <button onClick={() => dispatch({ type: "reset" })}>reset</button>
    </div>
  );
};
```

| /10 | -10 | -1 | 0 | +1 | +10 | *10 | reset |

https://codesandbox.io/s/redux-toolkit-createaction-createreducer-2-c2dpqf

Under the hood, createReducer() uses Immer, allowing you to mutate the state directly in your reducers.

In practice, a reducer should either return a new state or mutate the state in place, but not both.

/src/index.js
```
import React from "react";
import { createRoot } from "react-dom/client";
import { Provider } from "react-redux";
import store from "./store";
import App from "./App";

const root = createRoot(document.getElementById("root"));
root.render(
  <Provider store={store}>
    <App />
  </Provider>
);
```

/src/reducer.js
```
import { createAction, createReducer } from "@reduxjs/toolkit";

const initialState = { x: 0, y: 100 };
const plusX = createAction("plusX");
const plusY = createAction("plusY");

export { plusX, plusY };

export default createReducer(initialState, (builder) => {
  builder
    .addCase(plusX, (state, action) => {
      state.x += action.payload;
    })
    .addCase(plusY, (state, action) => {
      state.y += action.payload;
    })
    .addDefaultCase(() => initialState); // reset
});
```

/src/store.js
```
import reducer from "./reducer";
import { configureStore } from "@reduxjs/toolkit";

export default configureStore({
  reducer // ES6, ie.: reducer:reducer
});
```

/src/App.js

```
import { useSelector, useDispatch } from "react-redux";
import { plusX, plusY } from "./reducer";

export default () => {
  const v = useSelector((state) => state);
  const dispatch = useDispatch();
  return (
    <div>
      <button onClick={() => dispatch(plusY(-1))}>y-1</button>
      <button onClick={() => dispatch(plusX(-1))}>x-1</button>
      <span>
        ({v.x},{v.y})
      </span>
      <button onClick={() => dispatch(plusX(1))}>x+1</button>
      <button onClick={() => dispatch(plusY(1))}>y+1</button>
      <button onClick={() => dispatch({ type: "reset" })}>reset</button>
    </div>
  );
};
```

| y-1 | x-1 |(0,100)| x+1 | y+1 | reset |

https://codesandbox.io/s/redux-toolkit-createreducer-state-mutations-6l18mo

---

Multiple matchers may handle a single action, in the order they were defined,
after the case reducer ran.

/src/index.js
```
import React from "react";
import { createRoot } from "react-dom/client";
import { Provider } from "react-redux";
import store from "./store";
import App from "./App";

const root = createRoot(document.getElementById("root"));
root.render(
  <Provider store={store}>
    <App />
  </Provider>
);
```

/src/reducer.js
```
import { createAction, createReducer } from "@reduxjs/toolkit";

const initialState = 0;
const addAction = createAction("add1");
const plusAction = createAction("plus1");

export { plusAction, addAction };

export default createReducer(initialState, (builder) => {
  builder
    .addCase("plus1", (state) => state + 1)
    .addMatcher(
      (action) => action.type.endsWith("1"),
      (state) => state + 1
    )
    .addMatcher(
      (action) => action.type[0] === "p",
      (state) => state + 1
    );
});
```

/src/store.js
```
import reducer from "./reducer";
import { configureStore } from "@reduxjs/toolkit";
```

41

```
export default configureStore({
  reducer // ES6, ie.:  reducer:reducer
});
```

/src/App.js
```
import { useSelector, useDispatch } from "react-redux";
import { plusAction, addAction } from "./reducer";

export default () => {
  const v = useSelector((state) => state);
  const dispatch = useDispatch();
  return (
    <div>
      <span>{v}</span>
      <button onClick={() => dispatch(addAction())}>+1</button>
      <button onClick={() => dispatch(plusAction())}>+3</button>
    </div>
  );
};
```

0 +1 +3

https://codesandbox.io/s/redux-toolkit-createreducer-multiple-matchers-bwli7i

42

Immer makes it hard to log the state in a reducer. As a workaround, you can use current(), a function re-exported from Immer to Redux Toolkit.

/src/index.js
```
import React from "react";
import { createRoot } from "react-dom/client";
import { Provider } from "react-redux";
import store from "./store";
import App from "./App";

const root = createRoot(document.getElementById("root"));
root.render(
  <Provider store={store}>
    <App />
  </Provider>
);
```

/src/reducer.js
```
import { createAction, createReducer, current } from "@reduxjs/toolkit";

const initialState = { x: 0 };
const plusAction = createAction("plus1");

export { plusAction };

export default createReducer(initialState, (builder) => {
  builder.addCase(plusAction, (state) => {
    console.log(state); // Type Error
    console.log(current(state));
    state.x++;
  });
});
```

/src/store.js
```
import reducer from "./reducer";
import { configureStore } from "@reduxjs/toolkit";

export default configureStore({
  reducer // ES6, ie.:  reducer:reducer
});
```

/src/App.js
```
import { useSelector, useDispatch } from "react-redux";
import { plusAction } from "./reducer";

export default () => {
  const v = useSelector((state) => state);
  const dispatch = useDispatch();
  return (
    <div>
      <span>{v.x}</span>
      <button onClick={() => dispatch(plusAction())}>+1</button>
    </div>
  );
};
```

0 +1

https://codesandbox.io/s/redux-toolkit-createreducer-current-1cuunu

43

3.5. createSlice

Building on createAction() and createReducer(), createSlice() combines the definitions of action creators and reducers in one go, further simplifying the process:

If two fields from 'reducers' and 'extraReducers' happen to end up with the same action type string, the function from 'reducers' will be used to handle that action type.

/src/index.js
```
import React from "react";
import { createRoot } from "react-dom/client";
import { Provider } from "react-redux";
import store from "./store";
import App from "./App";

const root = createRoot(document.getElementById("root"));
root.render(
  <Provider store={store}>
    <App />
  </Provider>
);
```

/src/reducer.js
```
import { createSlice } from "@reduxjs/toolkit";

const initialState = { x: 0, y: 0 };

const counterSlice = createSlice({
  name: "counter",
  initialState,
  reducers: {
    // action creators to be auto-generated
    incrementX(state, action) {
      state.x += action.payload;
    },
    incrementY(state, action) {
      state.y += action.payload;
    }
  },
  extraReducers: (builder) => {
    builder
      .addMatcher(
        // divide10, multiply10
        (action) => action.type.endsWith("10"),
        (state, action) => {
          // mutations in place possible
          state.x = action.type[0] === "d" ? state.x / 10 : state.x * 10;
          state.y = action.type[0] === "d" ? state.y / 10 : state.y * 10;
        }
      )
      .addDefaultCase(() => initialState); // reset
  } /*,
  // alternative 'Map Object' notation, impossible to add matcher and default-case reducers
  extraReducers: {
    "counter/divide10": (state, action) => {
      state.x = state.x / 10;
      state.y = state.y / 10;
    },
    "counter/multiply10": (state) => {
      state.x = state.x * 10;
      state.y = state.y * 10;
    }
  }*/
});
```

```
console.log(counterSlice);
export const { incrementX, incrementY } = counterSlice.actions;
export default counterSlice.reducer;
```

/src/store.js
```
import reducer from "./reducer";
import { configureStore } from "@reduxjs/toolkit";

export default configureStore({
  reducer // ES6, ie.:  reducer:reducer
});
```

/src/App.js
```
import { useSelector, useDispatch } from "react-redux";
import { incrementX, incrementY } from "./reducer";

export default () => {
  const v = useSelector((state) => state);
  const dispatch = useDispatch();
  return (
    <div>
      <button onClick={() => dispatch(incrementX(-1))}>x-1</button>
      <button onClick={() => dispatch(incrementX(1))}>x+1</button>
      <span>
        ({v.x},{v.y})
      </span>
      <button onClick={() => dispatch(incrementY(-1))}>y-1</button>
      <button
        onClick={() => dispatch({ type: "counter/incrementY", payload: 1 })}
      >
        y+1
      </button>
      <br />
      <button onClick={() => dispatch({ type: "counter/multiply10" })}>
        *10
      </button>
      <button onClick={() => dispatch({ type: "reset" })}>reset</button>
    </div>
  );
};
```

| x-1 | x+1 | (0,0) | y-1 | y+1 |
| *10 | reset |

https://codesandbox.io/s/redux-toolkit-createslice-ks3i31

45

You can combine the reducers from multiple slices with the function combineReducer().

```
import { createSlice, createAction } from '@reduxjs/toolkit'
import { createStore, combineReducers } from 'redux'

const incrementBy = createAction('incrementBy')
const decrementBy = createAction('decrementBy')

const counter = createSlice({
  name: 'counter',
  initialState: 0,
  reducers: {
    increment: (state) => state + 1,
    decrement: (state) => state - 1,
    multiply: {
      reducer: (state, action) => state * action.payload,
      prepare: (value) => ({ payload: value || 2 }), // fallback if the payload is a falsy value
    },
  }
})
const user = createSlice({
  name: 'user',
  initialState: { name: '', age: 20 },
  reducers: {
    setUserName: (state, action) => {
      state.name = action.payload
    },
  }
});
const reducer = combineReducers({
  counter: counter.reducer,
  user: user.reducer,
});

const store = createStore(reducer);

store.dispatch(counter.actions.increment());
store.dispatch(counter.actions.increment());
store.dispatch(counter.actions.multiply(3));
store.dispatch(counter.actions.multiply());
console.log(`${counter.actions.decrement}`);
store.dispatch(user.actions.setUserName('eric'));
```

3.6.   createAsyncThunk

You should use a thunk if you want createSlice() to handle asynchronous operations.

createAsyncThunk() lets you define an action creator for an asynchronous operation, generating three other action creators ('/pending', '/fulfilled', '/rejected') in the process.

/src/index.js
```
import React from "react";
import { createRoot } from "react-dom/client";
import { Provider } from "react-redux";
import store from "./store";
import App from "./App";

const root = createRoot(document.getElementById("root"));
root.render(
  <Provider store={store}>
    <App />
  </Provider>
);
```

/src/reducer.js
```
import { createAsyncThunk, createSlice } from "@reduxjs/toolkit";

var tid;
function fetchMyData(i) {
 // simulating data fetching from server
 return new Promise((resolve, reject) => {
  tid = setTimeout(() => resolve(Math.random()), i * 1000);
  setTimeout(reject, 5000);
 });
}

const fetchData = createAsyncThunk(
  "data/fetchStatus",
  async (i, thunkAPI) => {
   //const state = thunkAPI.getState();
   //const extra = thunkAPI.extra;
   //const requestId = thunkAPI.requestId;
   //const signal = thunkAPI.signal;
   //console.log(state, extra, requestId, signal);
   //thunkAPI.dispatch({ type: "data/cancel" });
   //thunkAPI.rejectWithValue("rejected", { a: 0 });
   //thunkAPI.fulfillWithValue("fulfilled", { a: 0 });
   try {
     return await fetchMyData(i);
   } catch (err) {
     return thunkAPI.rejectWithValue("time out!");
   }
  },
  {
// condition: (arg, { getState, extra }) => true,
         // 'false' to prevent running payload creator
// dispatchConditionRejection: true,
         // 'true' to dispatch 'rejected' action when condition() returns 'false'
// idGenerator: ()=>Math.random(),
         // function generating 'requestId', defaults to nanoid()
// serializeError: console.error,
         // replaces the internal miniSerializeError method
// getPendingMeta: ({ arg, requestId }, { getState, extra })=>({})
         // creates an object that will be merged into the
         // pendingAction.meta field.
```

```
  }
);

const initialState = 0;

const dataSlice = createSlice({
  name: "data",
  initialState,
  reducers: {},
  extraReducers: (builder) => {
    builder
      .addCase(fetchData.pending, (state, action) => {
        console.log(action);
        clearTimeout(tid);
        return "fetching data...";
      })
      .addCase(fetchData.fulfilled, (state, action) => {
        console.log(action);
        return action.payload;
      })
      .addCase(fetchData.rejected, (state, action) => {
        console.log(action);
        if (action.meta.aborted) return "cancelled!";
        return action.payload;
      });
  }
});

export { fetchData };
export const { cancel } = dataSlice.actions;
export default dataSlice.reducer;
```

/src/store.js
```
import reducer from "./reducer";
import { configureStore } from "@reduxjs/toolkit";

export default configureStore({
  reducer // ES6, ie.:  reducer:reducer
});
```

/src/App.js
```
import { unwrapResult } from "@reduxjs/toolkit";
import { useRef } from "react";
import { useSelector, useDispatch } from "react-redux";
import { fetchData } from "./reducer";

export default () => {
  const v = useSelector((state) => state);
  const dispatch = useDispatch();
  const abort = useRef();
  return (
    <div>
      <span>{v}</span>
      <button
        onClick={() => {
          const d = dispatch(fetchData(3));
          abort.current = d.abort;
          d.then(() => console.log("resolved"));
        }}
      >
        Fetch Data
      </button>
      <button
        onClick={() => {
          const d = dispatch(fetchData(6));
```

```
        abort.current = d.abort;
        d.unwrap() // to extract the payload of a fulfilled action or to throw either the error or, if
                   // available, payload created by rejectWithValue from a rejected action
        // .then(unwrapResult)    // alternative to .unwrap()
        .then((originalPromiseResult) => {
          console.log("originalPromiseResult", originalPromiseResult);
        })
        .catch((rejectedValueOrSerializedError) => {
          console.log(
            "rejectedValueOrSerializedError",
            rejectedValueOrSerializedError
          );
        });
    }}
    >
      Fetch Data Slowly
    </button>
    <button onClick={() => abort.current()}>Cancel</button>
  </div>
 );
};
```

| 0 | Fetch Data | Fetch Data Slowly | Cancel |

https://codesandbox.io/s/redux-toolkit-createasyncthunk-i7uv93

You can call **signal.addEventListener('abort', callback)** to run a callback when promise.abort() was called. Additionally, the Boolean property **thunkAPI.signal.aborted** can be used to check whether the thunk has been aborted.

The **fetch** api of modern browsers supports AbortSignal:

```
import { createAsyncThunk } from '@reduxjs/toolkit'

const fetchUserById = createAsyncThunk(
  'users/fetchById',
  async (userId: string, thunkAPI) => {
    const response = await fetch(`https://reqres.in/api/users/${userId}`, {
      signal: thunkAPI.signal,
    })
    return await response.json()
  }
);
```

3.7. createEntityAdapter

So far we have been coding our reducer functions manually.

createEntityAdapter() automatically generates some helpful reducer functions (ie. CRUD operations) for us.

It normalizes the state into the form {ids: [], entities: {}}, where 'ids' stores the ids of the records/entities, and 'entities' maps each id to its corresponding record/entity.

> If updateMany() is called repeatedly to the same ID, they will be merged into a single update, with later updates overwriting the earlier ones.
> For both updateOne() and updateMany(), changing the ID of one existing entity to match the ID of a second existing entity will cause the first to replace the second completely.

/src/index.js
```
import React from "react";
import { createRoot } from "react-dom/client";
import { Provider } from "react-redux";
import store from "./store";
import App from "./App";

const root = createRoot(document.getElementById("root"));
root.render(
  <Provider store={store}>
    <App />
  </Provider>
);
```

/src/reducer.js
```
import { createEntityAdapter, createSlice, current } from "@reduxjs/toolkit";

const booksAdapter = createEntityAdapter({
  // Assume IDs are stored in a field other than `book.id`
  selectId: (book) => book.bookId,
  // Keep the "all IDs" array sorted based on book titles
  sortComparer: (a, b) => a.title.localeCompare(b.title)
});

const booksSlice = createSlice({
  name: "books",
  initialState: booksAdapter.getInitialState(),
  reducers: {
    // Can pass adapter functions directly as case reducers.
    // Because we're passing this as a value, `createSlice` will auto-generate the
    // `bookAdded` action type / creator
    addBook: booksAdapter.addOne,
    setBook: booksAdapter.setOne,
    add2Books: booksAdapter.addMany,
    log: (state, actions) => {
      const s = booksAdapter.getSelectors();
      console.log(1, current(s.selectIds(state)));
      console.log(2, s.selectAll(state));
      console.log(3, s.selectById(state, "x"));
      console.log(4, current(s.selectEntities(state)));
      console.log(5, s.selectTotal(state));
      return state;
    }
  }
});
```

```
export const { addBook, setBook, add2Books, log } = booksSlice.actions;
export default booksSlice.reducer;
```

/src/store.js
```
import reducer from "./reducer";
import { configureStore } from "@reduxjs/toolkit";

export default configureStore({
  reducer // ES6, ie.: reducer:reducer
});
```

/src/App.js
```
import { useSelector, useDispatch } from "react-redux";
import { useRef } from "react";
import { addBook, setBook, add2Books, log } from "./reducer";

export default () => {
  let v = useSelector((state) => state);
  const dispatch = useDispatch();
  const inp_id = useRef("");
  const inp_title = useRef("");
  console.log(v);
  const book = () => ({
    bookId: inp_id.current.value,
    title: inp_title.current.value
  });
  return (
    <div>
      <input ref={inp_id} value={v.bookId} placeholder="enter id here" />
      <input ref={inp_title} value={v.title} placeholder="enter title here" />
      <button onClick={() => dispatch(addBook(book()))}>Add Book</button>
      <button onClick={() => dispatch(setBook(book()))}>Set Book</button>
      <button
        onClick={() =>
          dispatch(
            add2Books([
              book(),
              { bookId: book().bookId + "2", title: book().title + "2" }
            ])
          )
        }
      >
        Add 2 Books
      </button>
      <button onClick={() => dispatch(log())}>Log</button>
    </div>
  );
};
```

| enter id here | enter title here | Add Book | Set Book | Add 2 Books | Log |

https://codesandbox.io/s/redux-toolkit-createentityadapter-y4441f

51

The available adapter functions are:

- **addOne**: accepts a single entity, and adds it if it's not already present.
- **addMany**: accepts an array of entities or an object in the shape of Record<EntityId, T>, and adds them if not already present.
- **setOne**: accepts a single entity and adds or replaces it.
- **setMany**: accepts an array of entities or an object in the shape of Record<EntityId, T>, and adds or replaces them.
- **setAll**: accepts an array of entities or an object in the shape of Record<EntityId, T>, and replaces all existing entities with the values in the array.
- **removeOne**: accepts a single entity ID value, and removes the entity with that ID if it exists.
- **removeMany**: accepts an array of entity ID values, and removes each entity with those IDs if they exist.
- **removeAll**: removes all entities from the entity state object.
- **updateOne**: accepts an "update object" containing an entity ID and an object containing one or more new field values to update inside a changes field, and performs a shallow update on the corresponding entity.
- **updateMany**: accepts an array of update objects, and performs shallow updates on all corresponding entities.
- **upsertOne**: accepts a single entity. If an entity with that ID exists, it will perform a shallow update and the specified fields will be merged into the existing entity, with any matching fields overwriting the existing values. If the entity does not exist, it will be added.
- **upsertMany**: accepts an array of entities or an object in the shape of Record<EntityId, T> that will be shallowly upserted.

3.8. createSelector & createDraftSafeSelector

createSelector() allows you to define memoized functions that can compute a value from the state.

> When you call a selector (eg. selectSum), Reselect will run ALL your input selectors (eg. selectX) with all of the arguments you gave and look at the returned values. If any of the results are === different than before, it will re-run the output selector, and pass in those results as the arguments. If all of the results of the input selectors are the same as the last time, it will skip re-running the output selector, and just return the cached final result from before.

/src/index.js
```js
import React from "react";
import { createRoot } from "react-dom/client";
import { Provider } from "react-redux";
import store from "./store";
import App from "./App";

const root = createRoot(document.getElementById("root"));
root.render(
  <Provider store={store}>
    <App />
  </Provider>
);
```

/src/reducer.js
```js
import { createSlice, createSelector } from "@reduxjs/toolkit";

const initialState = { x: 0, y: 0, z: 0 };

const counterSlice = createSlice({
  name: "data",
  initialState,
  reducers: {
    // action creators to be auto-generated
    incrementX(state, action) {
      state.x += action.payload;
    },
    incrementY(state, action) {
      state.y += action.payload;
    },
    incrementZ(state, action) {
      state.z += action.payload;
    }
  }
});
export const { incrementX, incrementY, incrementZ } = counterSlice.actions;
export default counterSlice.reducer;

// Try to define reusable selectors alongside their corresponding reducers.
// input selectors
const selectX = (state) => state.x;
const selectY = (state) => state.y;
const selectZ = (state) => state.z;

const selectSum = createSelector(
  [selectX, selectY, selectZ], // notation 1
  (x, y, z) => x + y + z
);
const selectProduct = createSelector(
  selectX, // notation 2
  selectY,
```

53

```
  selectZ,
  (x, y, z) => x * y * z
);
const selectMySum = createSelector(
  selectSum,
  selectProduct,
  (state, i) => i,
  (s, p, i) => s + p + i
);
export { selectSum, selectProduct, selectMySum };
```

/src/store.js
```
import reducer from "./reducer";
import { configureStore } from "@reduxjs/toolkit";

export default configureStore({
  reducer // ES6, ie.:  reducer:reducer
});
```

/src/App.js
```
import { useSelector, useDispatch } from "react-redux";
import {
  incrementX,
  incrementY,
  incrementZ,
  selectSum,
  selectProduct,
  selectMySum
} from "./reducer";

export default () => {
  const state = useSelector((state) => state);
  const sum = selectSum(state);
  const product = selectProduct(state);
  const mysum = selectMySum(state, 1000); // 1000 to be passed to all input selectors as second
arg
  const dispatch = useDispatch();
  return (
    <div>
      <button onClick={() => dispatch(incrementZ(-1))}>Z-1</button>
      <button onClick={() => dispatch(incrementY(-1))}>Y-1</button>
      <button onClick={() => dispatch(incrementX(-1))}>X-1</button>
      <span>
        ({state.x},{state.y},{state.z})
      </span>
      <button onClick={() => dispatch(incrementX(1))}>X+1</button>
      <button onClick={() => dispatch(incrementY(1))}>Y+1</button>
      <button onClick={() => dispatch(incrementZ(1))}>Z+1</button>
      <br />
      <span>sum: {sum}</span>
      <br />
      <span>product: {product}</span>
      <br />
      <span>my sum: {mysum}</span>
    </div>
  );
};
```

| Z-1 | Y-1 | X-1 | (0,0,0) | X+1 | Y+1 | Z+1 |

sum: 0

product: 0

my sum: 1000

https://codesandbox.io/s/redux-toolkit-createselector-y38ehd

A memoized selector that uses state => state as an input will force the selector to always recalculate.

For memoization to work across multiple components, you should create a unique instance of the selector per component, so that each instance keeps getting the same arguments consistently. Below, without useMemo() or useCallback(), the output selector will be executed on repeated rendering even when the attribute (eg. value={1}) remains the same. This is because the selector uses the results of another copy of the component (<Sum value={2}/>). Also, notice how the selector factory function 'makeSelectSum' is defined.

/src/index.js
```
import React from "react";
import { createRoot } from "react-dom/client";
import { Provider } from "react-redux";
import store from "./store";
import App from "./App";

const root = createRoot(document.getElementById("root"));
root.render(
  <Provider store={store}>
    <App />
  </Provider>
);
```

/src/reducer.js
```
import { createSlice, createSelector } from "@reduxjs/toolkit";

const initialState = 0;
const counterSlice = createSlice({
  name: "data",
  initialState,
  reducers: {
    // action creators to be auto-generated
    increment(state, action) {
      return state + 1;
    }
  }
});
export const { increment } = counterSlice.actions;
export default counterSlice.reducer;

// input selectors
const select10 = (state) => 10;

// a selector factory
const makeSelectSum = () =>
  createSelector([select10, (state, n) => n], (a, num) => {
    console.log("output selector called: " + num);
    return a + num;
  });
export { makeSelectSum };
```

/src/store.js
```
import reducer from "./reducer";
import { configureStore } from "@reduxjs/toolkit";

export default configureStore({
  reducer // ES6, ie.: reducer:reducer
});
```

/src/App.js
```
import { useMemo, useCallback } from "react";
```

```
import { useSelector, useDispatch } from "react-redux";
import { increment, makeSelectSum } from "./reducer";

function Sum({ value }) {
  console.log("re-redering <Sum>...");
  const selectSumMemo = useMemo(makeSelectSum, []);
  // const selectSumMemo = useCallback(makeSelectSum(), []);   // alternative
  const sum = useSelector((state) => selectSumMemo(state, value));
  return (
    <div>
      sum: {sum} (10+{value})
    </div>
  );
}

export default () => {
  const state = useSelector((state) => state);
  const dispatch = useDispatch();
  return (
    <div>
      <Sum value={1} />
      <Sum value={2} />
      <button onClick={() => dispatch(increment())}>
        change state and re-render
      </button>
    </div>
  );
};
```

sum: 11 (10+1)

sum: 12 (10+2)

```
change state and re-render
```

https://codesandbox.io/s/
redux-toolkit-createselector-with-usememo-or-usecallback-4hmz97

In addition to a "globalized" selector, you may also use a "localized" selector, which accepts only a piece of the state as an argument, without knowing or caring where that is in the root state.

createDraftSafeSelector() allows you to create selectors that can safely be used inside of createReducer() and createSlice() reducers with Immer-powered mutable logic. All selectors created by entityAdapter.getSelectors() are "draft safe" selectors by default.

'unsafe1' and 'unsafe2' will be of the same value because the memoized selector was executed on the same object - but safe2 will be different from safe1 (with the updated value of 2), because the safe selector detected that it was executed on a Immer draft object and recalculated using the current value instead of returning a cached value.

```
const selectSelf = state => state
const unsafeSelector = createSelector(selectSelf, (state) => state.value)
const draftSafeSelector = createDraftSafeSelector(
  selectSelf,
  (state) => state.value
)

// in your reducer:

state.value = 1

const unsafe1 = unsafeSelector(state)
const safe1 = draftSafeSelector(state)

state.value = 2

const unsafe2 = unsafeSelector(state)
const safe2 = draftSafeSelector(state)
```

3.9. Matching Utilities

So far we have seen how isAnyOf() can be used in the matcher of a listener middleware.

Redux Toolkit exports several other matching utilities that you can leverage to check for specific kinds of actions. These are primarily useful for writing the builder.addMatcher() cases in createSlice and createReducer, as well as custom middleware.:

- **isAllOf** - returns true when all conditions are met
- **isAnyOf** - returns true when at least one of the conditions are met
- **isAsyncThunkAction** - accepts one or more action creators and returns true when all match
- **isPending** - accepts one or more action creators and returns true when all match
- **isFulfilled** - accepts one or more action creators and returns true when all match
- **isRejected** - accepts one or more action creators and returns true when all match
- **isRejectedWithValue** - accepts one or more action creators and returns true when all match

---

All 'thunk matchers' can either be called with one or more thunks as arguments, in which case they will return a matcher function for that condition and thunks, or with one action, in which case they will match for any thunk action with said condition.

(see official example at:
https://codesandbox.io/s/redux-toolkit-matchers-example-e765q)

---

4. Redux Toolkit Query

Redux Toolkit Query extends the functionality of Redux to the back end by fetching data from the server and storing it into the state locally.

It caches the results so that an identical request in future will not trigger unnecessary fetching.

Overview: (usage to be explained in detail in the latter sections)

Root APIs
- createApi({})
- fetchBaseQuery({})
- <ApiProvider>
- setupListeners()
- buildCreateApi
- coreModule
- reactHooksModule
- retry

Argument Keys to createApi({})
- baseQuery
- endpoints
- extractRehydrationInfo
- tagTypes
- reducerPath
- serializeQueryArgs
- keepUnusedDataFor
- refetchOnMountOrArgChange
- refetchOnFocus
- refetchOnReconnect

Member functions of createApi({}) endpoints builder
- query
- mutation

Argument Keys to createApi({}) endpoints builder
- query
- queryFn
- transformResponse
- extraOptions
- providesTags
- invalidatesTags
- keepUnusedDataFor
- onQueryStarted
- onCacheEntryAdded

Object keys of return slice of createApi({})
- reducerPath
- reducer
- middleware
- endpoints.{x}.initiate
- endpoints.{x}.select
- endpoints.{x}.matchPending
- endpoints.{x}.matchFulfilled
- endpoints.{x}.matchRejected
- injectEndpoints
- enhanceEndpoints
- utils.updateQueryData
- utils.patchQueryData
- utils.prefetch
- utils.invalidateTags
- utils.resetApiState
- utils.getRunningOperationPromises
- utils.getRunningOperationPromise
- internalActions
- [GeneratedReactHooks]

Generated React Hooks in slice
- use[Lazy]Query[Subscription]
- useQueryState
- useMutation
- usePrefetch

Hook Options
- skip
- pollingInterval
- selectFromResult
- refetchOnMountOrArgChange
- refechOnFocus
- refetchOnReconnect
- fixedCacheKey

Keys to object returned from calling Generated React Hooks
- data
- currentData
- error
- isUnintialized
- isLoading
- isFetching
- isSuccess
- isError
- refetch

60

Argument keys to fetchBaseQuery({})
- baseUrl
- prepareHeaders
- paramsSerializer
- fetchFn

Arguments to setupListeners()
- dispatch
- customHandler(dispatch, { onFocus, onFocusLost, onOffline, onOnline })

The following PHP scripts and data file will be used in the subsequent examples in this chapter. The front parts of the two PHP scripts are meant to allow cross-origin resource sharing (CORS). Then, 'get_post.php' returns the text in the data file, while 'update_post.php' randomizes the cases (upper/lower) of the letters of the text in the date file and returns the new content.

```php
<?php
// /myserver.com/get_post.php
header('Access-Control-Allow-Origin: *');
header('Access-Control-Allow-Methods: GET, PUT, POST, DELETE, OPTIONS, post, get');
header("Access-Control-Max-Age", "3600");
header('Access-Control-Allow-Headers: Origin, Content-Type, X-Auth-Token');
header("Access-Control-Allow-Credentials", "true");
sleep(1);
echo json_encode(array("post"=>file_get_contents("data".$_GET["id"].".txt")));
?>
```

```php
<?php
// /myserver.com/update_post.php
header('Access-Control-Allow-Origin: *');
header("Access-Control-Allow-Methods: HEAD, GET, POST, PUT, PATCH, DELETE, OPTIONS");
header("Access-Control-Allow-Headers: X-API-KEY, Origin, X-Requested-With, Content-Type,
Accept, Access-Control-Request-Method,Access-Control-Request-Headers, Authorization");
header('Content-Type: application/json');
if ($_SERVER['REQUEST_METHOD'] == "OPTIONS") {
   header('Access-Control-Allow-Origin: *');
   header("Access-Control-Allow-Headers: X-API-KEY, Origin, X-Requested-With, Content-Type,
Accept, Access-Control-Request-Method,Access-Control-Request-Headers, Authorization");
   header("HTTP/1.1 200 OK");
   die();
}
$str="HELLO WORLD";
$r="";
for ($i = 0; $i < strlen($str); $i++){
  if (rand(0,100)>50) $r .= strtoupper($str[$i]);
  else                $r .= strtolower($str[$i]);
}
$data = json_decode(file_get_contents('php://input'), true);
if ($data["id"]=="1") file_put_contents("data1.txt",$r);
echo json_encode(array("post"=>$r,"serverMessage"=>"done!!"));
?>
```

```
/myserver.com/data1.txt
HELLO WORLD
```

Because CodeSandbox does not support PHP, the corresponding PHP files on CodeSandbox will return dummy JSON data instead.

4.1. Query

The most important function in Redux Toolkit Query, createApi() returns a slice with members that you can mount to your redux store, as well as hooks that you can use to fetch data from the defined endpoints.

Notice how the hook useGetPostQuery() is automatically generated from the endpoint 'getPost'.

/src/index.js
```
import React from "react";
import { createRoot } from "react-dom/client";
import { Provider } from "react-redux";
import { store } from "./store";
import { App } from "./App";

const root = createRoot(document.getElementById("root"));

root.render(
  <Provider store={store}>
    <App />
  </Provider>
);
```

/src/store/index.js
```
import { configureStore } from "@reduxjs/toolkit";
// Or from '@reduxjs/toolkit/query/react'
import { setupListeners } from "@reduxjs/toolkit/query";
import { postApi } from "./postApi";

export const store = configureStore({
  reducer: {
    // Add the generated reducer as a specific top-level slice
    [postApi.reducerPath]: postApi.reducer
  },
  // Adding the api middleware enables caching, invalidation, polling,
  // and other useful features of `rtk-query`.
  middleware: (getDefaultMiddleware) =>
    getDefaultMiddleware().concat(postApi.middleware)
});

// optional, but required for refetchOnFocus/refetchOnReconnect behaviors
// see `setupListeners` docs - takes an optional callback as the 2nd arg for
// customization
setupListeners(store.dispatch);
```

/src/store/postApi.js
```
import { createApi, fetchBaseQuery } from "@reduxjs/toolkit/query/react";

export const postApi = createApi({
  reducerPath: "postApi",
  baseQuery: fetchBaseQuery({ baseUrl: "https://myserver.com/" }),
  endpoints: (builder) => ({
    getPost: builder.query({
      query: (id) => `get_post.php?id=${id}` // expects a JSON response
    })
  })
});

// Export hooks for usage in functional components, which are
// auto-generated based on the defined endpoints
export const { useGetPostQuery } = postApi;
```

/src/App.js
```
import { useGetPostQuery } from "./store/postApi";

export function App() {
```

```
const { data, isLoading, isFetching, isError, error } = useGetPostQuery(1);
if (isError)
  return (
    <div>
      {error.status}
      <br />
      {error.data}
    </div>
  );
if (isLoading) return <div>loading...</div>;
return <div className={isFetching ? "posts--disabled" : ""}>
      {data.post}</div>;
}
```

hELLO WORLD

https://codesandbox.io/s/redux-toolkit-query-basic-query-35qdxf

---

If you don't want to automatically trigger the query request, you should use
useLazyQuery() instead of useQuery().

/src/index.js
```
import React from "react";
import { createRoot } from "react-dom/client";
import { Provider } from "react-redux";
import { store } from "./store";
import { App } from "./App";

const root = createRoot(document.getElementById("root"));

root.render(
  <Provider store={store}>
    <App />
  </Provider>
);
```

/src/store/index.js
```
import { configureStore } from "@reduxjs/toolkit";
// Or from '@reduxjs/toolkit/query/react'
import { setupListeners } from "@reduxjs/toolkit/query";
import { postApi } from "./postApi";

export const store = configureStore({
  reducer: {
    // Add the generated reducer as a specific top-level slice
    [postApi.reducerPath]: postApi.reducer
  },
  // Adding the api middleware enables caching, invalidation, polling,
  // and other useful features of `rtk-query`.
  middleware: (getDefaultMiddleware) =>
    getDefaultMiddleware().concat(postApi.middleware)
});

// optional, but required for refetchOnFocus/refetchOnReconnect behaviors
// see `setupListeners` docs - takes an optional callback as the 2nd arg for
// customization
setupListeners(store.dispatch);
```

/src/store/postApi.js
```
import { createApi, fetchBaseQuery } from "@reduxjs/toolkit/query/react";

export const postApi = createApi({
  reducerPath: "postApi",
  baseQuery: fetchBaseQuery(
```

```
                    { baseUrl: "https://myserver.com/" }),
  endpoints: (builder) => ({
    getPost: builder.query({
      query: (id) => `get_post.php?id=${id}` // expects a JSON response
    })
  })
});

export const { useLazyGetPostQuery } = postApi;
```

/src/App.js
```
import { useLazyGetPostQuery } from "./store/postApi";

export function App() {
  const [trigger, result, lastPromiseInfo] = useLazyGetPostQuery();
  console.log(result, lastPromiseInfo);
  if (result.status === "uninitialized") {
    return <button onClick={() => trigger(1)}>Fetch Post</button>;
  } else {
    const { data, error, isError, isLoading, isFetching } = result;
    if (isError)
      return (
        <div>
          {error.status}
          <br />
          {error.data}
        </div>
      );
    if (isLoading) return <div>loading...</div>;
    return (
      <div className={isFetching ? "posts--disabled" : ""}>{data.post}</div>
    );
  }
}
```

| Fetch Post |

https://codesandbox.io/s/redux-toolkit-query-uselazyquery-4p2r7m

isLoading refers to a query being in flight for the first time for the given hook. No data will be available at this time.

isFetching refers to a query being in flight for the given endpoint + query param combination, but not necessarily for the first time. Data may be available from an earlier request done by this hook, maybe with the previous query param.

You can split the operation of useQuery() into two steps: useQueryState() and useQuerySubscription(), which are accessible via api.endpoints.
The hook useLazyQuerySubscription() also exists.

/src/index.js

```
import React from "react";
import { createRoot } from "react-dom/client";
import { Provider } from "react-redux";
import { store } from "./store";
import { App } from "./App";

const root = createRoot(document.getElementById("root"));

root.render(
  <Provider store={store}>
    <App />
  </Provider>
);
```

/src/store/index.js

```
import { configureStore } from "@reduxjs/toolkit";
// Or from '@reduxjs/toolkit/query/react'
import { setupListeners } from "@reduxjs/toolkit/query";
import { postApi } from "./postApi";

export const store = configureStore({
  reducer: {
    // Add the generated reducer as a specific top-level slice
    [postApi.reducerPath]: postApi.reducer
  },
  // Adding the api middleware enables caching, invalidation, polling,
  // and other useful features of `rtk-query`.
  middleware: (getDefaultMiddleware) =>
    getDefaultMiddleware().concat(postApi.middleware)
});

// optional, but required for refetchOnFocus/refetchOnReconnect behaviors
// see `setupListeners` docs - takes an optional callback as the 2nd arg for
// customization
setupListeners(store.dispatch);
```

/src/store/postApi.js

```
import { createApi, fetchBaseQuery } from "@reduxjs/toolkit/query/react";

export const postApi = createApi({
  reducerPath: "postApi",
  baseQuery: fetchBaseQuery(
                          { baseUrl: "https://myserver.com/" }),
  endpoints: (builder) => ({
    getPost: builder.query({
      query: (id) => `get_post.php?id=${id}` // expects a JSON response
    })
  })
});
export const useGetPostState = postApi.**endpoints.getPost.useQueryState**;
export const useGetPostQuerySubscription =
  postApi.**endpoints.getPost.useQuerySubscription**;
```

/src/App.js

```
import { useGetPostState, useGetPostQuerySubscription } from "./store/postApi";

export function App() {
  const { refetch } = useGetPostQuerySubscription(1); // initiates actual fetching
  const { data, isLoading, isFetching, isUninitialized } = useGetPostState(1);
  console.log(data, isUninitialized, isLoading, isFetching);
  if (isLoading) return <div>loading...</div>;
  if (isFetching) return <div>fetching...</div>;
```

```
  return (
    <div>
      {data ? data.post : ""}
      <button onClick={refetch}>Refetch</button>
    </div>
  );
}
```

hELLO WORLD Refetch

https://codesandbox.io/s/
redux-toolkit-query-usequerystate-and-usequerysubscription-h326y7

An options object may be passed as the second argument to the hooks
useQuery[State|Subscription](), or as the only argument to
useLazyQuery[Subscription]().

Eg. This creates a real-time effect:

```
useGetPostQuery(123,{pollingInterval:30000});
```

option key	use Query	use QueryState	use QuerySubscription	use LazyQuery	use LazyQuery Subscription
pollingInterval: number (0) The interval in milliseconds to poll for (refetch) the data.	√		√	√	√
refetchOnReconnect: boolean (false) Allows forcing the query to refetch when regaining a network connection.	√		√	√	√
refetchOnFocus: boolean (false) Allows forcing the query to refetch when the browser window regains focus.	√		√	√	√
skip: boolean (false) Allows a query to 'skip' running for that render.	√	√	√		
refetchOnMountOrArgChange : boolean | number (false) Allows forcing the query to always refetch on mount (when true is provided). Allows forcing the query to refetch if enough time (in seconds) has passed since the last query for the same cache (when a number is provided).	√		√		
selectFromResult: (result: UseQueryStateDefaultResult) => any Allows altering the returned value of the hook to obtain a subset of the result, render-optimized for the returned subset.	√	√		√	

If the selected item is one element in a larger collection, it will disregard
changes to the other elements in the same collection when deciding whether to
re-render.

/src/index.js

```
import React from "react";
import { createRoot } from "react-dom/client";
import { Provider } from "react-redux";
import { store } from "./store";
import { App } from "./App";

const root = createRoot(document.getElementById("root"));

root.render(
  <Provider store={store}>
    <App />
  </Provider>
);
```

/src/store/index.js
```
import { configureStore } from "@reduxjs/toolkit";
// Or from '@reduxjs/toolkit/query/react'
import { setupListeners } from "@reduxjs/toolkit/query";
import { postApi } from "./postApi";

export const store = configureStore({
  reducer: {
    // Add the generated reducer as a specific top-level slice
    [postApi.reducerPath]: postApi.reducer
  },
  // Adding the api middleware enables caching, invalidation, polling,
  // and other useful features of `rtk-query`.
  middleware: (getDefaultMiddleware) =>
    getDefaultMiddleware().concat(postApi.middleware)
});

setupListeners(store.dispatch);
```

/src/store/postApi.js
```
import { createApi, fetchBaseQuery } from "@reduxjs/toolkit/query/react";

export const postApi = createApi({
  reducerPath: "postApi",
  baseQuery: fetchBaseQuery({ baseUrl: "https://myserver.com/" }),
  endpoints: (builder) => ({
    getPost: builder.query({
      query: (id) => `get_post.php?id=${id}` // expects a JSON response
    })
  })
});
export const { useGetPostQuery } = postApi;
```

/src/App.js
```
import { useGetPostQuery } from "./store/postApi";
export function App() {
  const { post } = useGetPostQuery(1, {
    selectFromResult: ({ data }) => ({ post: data ? data.post : "loading..." })
  });
  return <div>{post}</div>;
}
```

hELLO WORLD

https://codesandbox.io/s/redux-toolkit-query-selectfromresult-fzi16f

As a shallow equality check is used to decide whether to re-render the component, you should try to reference the same object (eg. an empty array assigned to a variable externally) if you want to enjoy the associated performance benefits. Also, consider using createSelector().

```
// An array declared here will maintain a stable reference rather than be re-created again
const emptyArray: Post[] = []
```

```
function PostsList() {
  // This call will result in an initial render returning an empty array for `posts`,
  // and a second render when the data is received.
  // It will trigger additional rerenders only if the `posts` data changes
  const { posts } = api.useGetPostsQuery(undefined, {
    selectFromResult: ({ data }) => ({
      posts: data ?? emptyArray,
    }),
  })

  return (
    <ul>
      {posts.map((post) => (
        <PostById key={post.id} id={post.id} />
      ))}
    </ul>
  )
}
```

'queryFn' can be used in place of 'query' to bypass baseQuery. Here, we deliberately create two somewhat identical endpoints for comparison. You must specify one of the two keys ('query' or 'queryFn') but not both for an endpoint. Notice how the 'query' response is transformed.

/src/index.js
```
import React from "react";
import { createRoot } from "react-dom/client";
import { Provider } from "react-redux";
import { store } from "./store";
import { App } from "./App";

const root = createRoot(document.getElementById("root"));

root.render(
  <Provider store={store}>
    <App />
  </Provider>
);
```

/src/store/index.js
```
import { configureStore } from "@reduxjs/toolkit";
// Or from '@reduxjs/toolkit/query/react'
import { setupListeners } from "@reduxjs/toolkit/query";
import { postApi } from "./postApi";

export const store = configureStore({
  reducer: {
    // Add the generated reducer as a specific top-level slice
    [postApi.reducerPath]: postApi.reducer
  },
  // Adding the api middleware enables caching, invalidation, polling,
  // and other useful features of `rtk-query`.
  middleware: (getDefaultMiddleware) =>
    getDefaultMiddleware().concat(postApi.middleware)
});
setupListeners(store.dispatch);
```

/src/store/postApi.js
```
import { createApi, fetchBaseQuery } from "@reduxjs/toolkit/query/react";

export const postApi = createApi({
  reducerPath: "postApi",
  baseQuery: fetchBaseQuery({ baseUrl: "https://myserver.com/" }),
  endpoints: (builder) => ({
    getPost: builder.query({
      query: (id) => `get_post.php?id=${id}`, // expects a JSON response
      transformResponse: (response, meta, arg) => {
        // not applicable to queryFn
        console.log("meta", meta);
        return { post: response.post.toLowerCase() };
      }
    }),
    getPostFn: builder.query({
      queryFn(arg, queryApi, extraOptions, baseQuery) {
        console.log("queryApi", queryApi);
        if (Math.random() < 0.9) {
          return fetch(
            `https://myserver.com/${extraOptions.file}?id=${arg}`
          )
            .then((r) => r.json())
            .then((j) => ({ data: j }));
        } else
          return {
            error: {
```

69

```
            status: 500,
            statusText: "Internal Server Error",
            data: "Just a simulated error!"
          }
        };
      },
      extraOptions: { file: "get_post.php" }
    })
  })
});

// Export hooks for usage in functional components, which are
// auto-generated based on the defined endpoints
export const { useGetPostQuery, useGetPostFnQuery } = postApi;
```

/src/App.js
```
import { useGetPostQuery, useGetPostFnQuery } from "./store/postApi";

export function App() {
  const { data, isLoading } = useGetPostQuery(1);
  const result = useGetPostFnQuery(1);
  console.log("result", result);
  return (
    <div>
      {isLoading ? <div>loading...</div> : <div>{data.post}</div>}
      {result.isLoading ? <div>loading...</div> :
                          <div>{result.data.post}</div>}
    </div>
  );
}
```

hello world

hELLO WORLD

https://codesandbox.io/s/redux-toolkit-query-queryfn-and-extraoptions-j89cvp

4.2. Mutation

A 'mutation' modifies data in the server.

Unlike the useQuery hook, the useMutation hook doesn't execute automatically. Here, 'getPost' will refetch when any of its provided tags gets invalidated.

/src/index.js
```
import React from "react";
import { createRoot } from "react-dom/client";
import { Provider } from "react-redux";
import { store } from "./store";
import { App } from "./App";

const root = createRoot(document.getElementById("root"));

root.render(
  <Provider store={store}>
    <App />
  </Provider>
);
```

/src/store/index.js
```
import { configureStore } from "@reduxjs/toolkit";
// Or from '@reduxjs/toolkit/query/react'
import { setupListeners } from "@reduxjs/toolkit/query";
import { postApi } from "./postApi";

export const store = configureStore({
  reducer: {
    // Add the generated reducer as a specific top-level slice
    [postApi.reducerPath]: postApi.reducer
  },
  // Adding the api middleware enables caching, invalidation, polling,
  // and other useful features of `rtk-query`.
  middleware: (getDefaultMiddleware) =>
    getDefaultMiddleware().concat(postApi.middleware)
});

setupListeners(store.dispatch);
```

/src/store/postApi.js
```
import { createApi, fetchBaseQuery } from "@reduxjs/toolkit/query/react";

export const postApi = createApi({
  reducerPath: "postApi",
  baseQuery: fetchBaseQuery({
    baseUrl: "https://myserver.com/"
  }),
  tagTypes: ["Posts"],
  endpoints: (builder) => ({
    getPost: builder.query({
      query: (id) => `get_post.php?id=${id}`, // expects a JSON response
      providesTags: (result, error, id) => [{ type: "Posts", id }]
    }),
    updatePost: builder.mutation({
      query: (body) => {
        console.log("body", body);
        return {
          url: `update_post.php`,
          method: "POST",
          body
        };
      },
      invalidatesTags: (result, error, { id }) => [{ type: "Posts", id }]
    })
```

```
  })
});

// Export hooks for usage in functional components, which are
// auto-generated based on the defined endpoints
export const { useGetPostQuery, useUpdatePostMutation } = postApi;
```

```
/src/App.js
import { useGetPostQuery, useUpdatePostMutation } from "./store/postApi";

export function App() {
  const { data, isFetching } = useGetPostQuery(1);
  const [
    updatePost, // This is the mutation trigger
    { isLoading } // This is the destructured mutation result
  ] = useUpdatePostMutation();
  console.log("rendering <App>"); // 1.isFetching 2.isLoading 3.data
  return (
    <div>
      {isFetching || isLoading ? "loading..." : data.post}
      <button onClick={() => updatePost({ id: 1 })}>mutate</button>
    </div>
  );
}
```

hELLO WORLD mutate

https://codesandbox.io/s/redux-toolkit-query-mutation-t7zx8d

Note that the 'id' field of a cache tag is optional.

Invalidating ['Post'] will invalidate cache entries with these tags:
- ['Post']
- [{ type: 'Post' }]
- [{ type: 'Post', id: 1 }, { type: 'User' }]
- [{ type: 'Post', id: 1 }, { type: 'Post', id: 'LIST' }]

You can also define cache tags for errors:

```
import { createApi, fetchBaseQuery } from '@reduxjs/toolkit/query'
const api = createApi({
  baseQuery: fetchBaseQuery({ baseUrl: 'https://example.com' }),
  tagTypes: ['Post', 'UNAUTHORIZED', 'UNKNOWN_ERROR'],
  endpoints: (build) => ({
    postById: build.query({
      query: (id) => `post/${id}`,
      providesTags: (result, error, id) =>
        result
          ? [{ type: 'Post', id }]
          : error?.status === 401
          ? ['UNAUTHORIZED']
          : ['UNKNOWN_ERROR'],
    }),
    login: build.mutation({
      query: () => '/login',
      // on successful login, will refetch all currently
      // 'UNAUTHORIZED' queries
      invalidatesTags: (result) => (result ? ['UNAUTHORIZED'] : []),
    }),
    refetchErroredQueries: build.mutation({
      queryFn: () => ({ data: null }),
      invalidatesTags: ['UNKNOWN_ERROR'],
    }),
  }),
})
```

In this example, we do away with useQuery() and tags, showing how we can potentially make optimistic updates on the UI with onQueryStarted(). Realize that the server response can be retrieved via updateResult (.data and .unwrap()) too.

In an optimistic update the UI behaves as though a change was successfully completed before receiving confirmation from the server that it actually was - it is being optimistic that it will eventually get the confirmation rather than an error. This allows for a more responsive user experience.

/src/index.js
```
import React from "react";
import { createRoot } from "react-dom/client";
import { Provider } from "react-redux";
import { store } from "./store";
import { App } from "./App";

const root = createRoot(document.getElementById("root"));

root.render(
  <Provider store={store}>
    <App />
  </Provider>
);
```

/src/store/index.js
```
import { configureStore } from "@reduxjs/toolkit";
// Or from '@reduxjs/toolkit/query/react'
import { setupListeners } from "@reduxjs/toolkit/query";
import { postApi } from "./postApi";

export const store = configureStore({
  reducer: {
    // Add the generated reducer as a specific top-level slice
    [postApi.reducerPath]: postApi.reducer,
```

```
    post: function (state = "???", action) {
      switch (action.type) {
        case "LOADING":
          return "loading...";
        case "READY":
          return action.post;
        default:
          return state;
      }
    }
  },
  // Adding the api middleware enables caching, invalidation, polling,
  // and other useful features of `rtk-query`.
  middleware: (getDefaultMiddleware) =>
    getDefaultMiddleware().concat(postApi.middleware)
});

// optional, but required for refetchOnFocus/refetchOnReconnect behaviors
// see `setupListeners` docs - takes an optional callback as the 2nd arg for
// customization
setupListeners(store.dispatch);
```

/src/store/postApi.js
```
import { createApi, fetchBaseQuery } from "@reduxjs/toolkit/query/react";

export const postApi = createApi({
  reducerPath: "postApi",
  baseQuery: fetchBaseQuery({
    baseUrl: "https://myserver.com/"
  }),
  endpoints: (builder) => ({
    updatePost: builder.mutation({
      query: (body) => {
        return {
          url: `update_post.php`,
          method: "POST",
          body
        };
      },
      async onQueryStarted( // onQueryStarted is useful for optimistic updates
        arg,
        { dispatch, getState, queryFulfilled, requestId, extra, getCacheEntry }
      ) {
        console.log("cache entry", getCacheEntry());
        dispatch({ type: "LOADING" });
      },
      async onCacheEntryAdded(
        arg,
        {
          dispatch,
          getState,
          extra,
          requestId,
          cacheEntryRemoved,
          cacheDataLoaded,
          getCacheEntry
        }
      ) {
        const serverResponse = (await cacheDataLoaded).data;
        console.log("payload (cacheDataLoaded):", serverResponse);
        dispatch({ type: "READY", post: serverResponse.post });
      }
    })
```

74

```
    })
  });
export const { useGetPostQuery, useUpdatePostMutation } = postApi;
```

```
/src/App.js
import { useUpdatePostMutation } from "./store/postApi";
import { useSelector } from "react-redux";

export function App() {
  const post = useSelector((s) => s.post);
  const [
    updatePost, // This is the mutation trigger
    updateResult // This is the mutation result
  ] = useUpdatePostMutation();
  console.log("rendering <App>...updateResult:", updateResult);
  return (
    <div>
      {post}
      <button
        onClick={() => {
          updatePost({ id: 1 })
          .unwrap() // abort() unsubscribe() reset()
          .then((payload) => console.log("payload (unwrap())", payload));
        }}
      >
        mutate
      </button>
      <br />
      <br />
      <button onClick={() => updateResult.reset()}>
        reset the hook back to it's original state and remove the current result
        from the cache
      </button>
    </div>
  );
}
```

??? `mutate`

`reset the hook back to it's original state and remove the current result from the cache`

https://codesandbox.io/s/redux-toolkit-query-optimistic-update-ti3z4q

75

You can share results across mutation hook instances using the 'fixedCacheKey' option.

You can also define the 'selectFromResult' option as you see in the previous section.

/src/index.js
```
import React from "react";
import { createRoot } from "react-dom/client";
import { Provider } from "react-redux";
import { store } from "./store";
import { App } from "./App";

const root = createRoot(document.getElementById("root"));

root.render(
  <Provider store={store}>
    <App />
  </Provider>
);
```

/src/store/index.js
```
import { configureStore } from "@reduxjs/toolkit";
// Or from '@reduxjs/toolkit/query/react'
import { setupListeners } from "@reduxjs/toolkit/query";
import { postApi } from "./postApi";

export const store = configureStore({
  reducer: {
    // Add the generated reducer as a specific top-level slice
    [postApi.reducerPath]: postApi.reducer
  },
  // Adding the api middleware enables caching, invalidation, polling,
  // and other useful features of `rtk-query`.
  middleware: (getDefaultMiddleware) =>
    getDefaultMiddleware().concat(postApi.middleware)
});
setupListeners(store.dispatch);
```

/src/store/postApi.js
```
import { createApi, fetchBaseQuery } from "@reduxjs/toolkit/query/react";

export const postApi = createApi({
  reducerPath: "postApi",
  baseQuery: fetchBaseQuery({
    baseUrl: "https://myserver.com/"
  }),
  endpoints: (builder) => ({
    updatePost: builder.mutation({
      query: (body) => {
        return {
          url: `update_post.php`,
          method: "POST",
          body
        };
      }
    })
  })
});

// Export hooks for usage in functional components, which are
// auto-generated based on the defined endpoints
export const { useGetPostQuery, useUpdatePostMutation } = postApi;
```

/src/App.js
```
import { useUpdatePostMutation } from "./store/postApi";
```

```
function Component1() {
  const [updatePost, updateResult] = useUpdatePostMutation({
    fixedCacheKey: "shared-post" // result will be reflected in <Component2>
  });
  console.log("rendering <Component1>");
  return (
    <div>
      {updateResult.data ? updateResult.data.post : "???"}
      <button onClick={() => updatePost({ id: 1 })}>mutate</button>
    </div>
  );
}

function Component2() {
  const [updatePost, updateResult] = useUpdatePostMutation({
    fixedCacheKey: "shared-post" // result will be reflected in <Component1>
  });
  console.log("rendering <Component2>");
  return (
    <div>
      {updateResult.data ? updateResult.data.post : "???"}
      <button onClick={() => updatePost({ id: 1 })}>mutate</button>
    </div>
  );
}

export function App() {
  return (
    <div>
      <Component1 />
      <Component2 />
    </div>
  );
}
```

??? mutate

??? mutate

https://codesandbox.io/s/redux-toolkit-query-fixedcachekey-721ok2

Tip 1: you can easily implement pagination by passing a 'page' state to a query hook and invalidating the cache tags for the pages when a deletion occurs.

Tip 2: To stream updates, you can combine a mutation with a Web Socket:

```
import { createApi, fetchBaseQuery } from '@reduxjs/toolkit/query/react'
import { isMessage } from './schemaValidators'
export const api = createApi({
  baseQuery: fetchBaseQuery({ baseUrl: '/' }),
  endpoints: (build) => ({
    getMessages: build.query({
      query: (channel) => `messages/${channel}`,
      async onCacheEntryAdded(
        arg,
        { updateCachedData, cacheDataLoaded, cacheEntryRemoved }
      ) {
        const ws = new WebSocket('ws://localhost:8080')
                        // create a websocket connection when the cache subscription starts
        try {
          await cacheDataLoaded   // wait for the initial query to resolve before proceeding

          // when data is received from the socket connection to the server,
          // if it is a message and for the appropriate channel,
          // update our query result with the received message
          const listener = (event) => {
            const data = JSON.parse(event.data)
            if (!isMessage(data) || data.channel !== arg) return
            b((draft) => {
              draft.push(data)
            })
          }
          ws.addEventListener('message', listener)
        } catch {
          // no-op in case `cacheEntryRemoved` resolves before `cacheDataLoaded`,
          // in which case `cacheDataLoaded` will throw
        }
        await cacheEntryRemoved
                    // cacheEntryRemoved will resolve when the cache subscription is no longer active
        ws.close()   // perform cleanup steps once the `cacheEntryRemoved` promise resolves
      },
    }),
  }),
})
export const { useGetMessagesQuery } = api
```

4.3. Unsubscribing

When all the components that subscribe to a query have been unmounted, the cache entry associated with the query is removed after some time (default to 60s).

Consider this:

> Below, if 'conditionA' is true, three cache entries will be created (for useGetUserQuery(1), useGetUserQuery(2), and useGetUserQuery(3)). If at a later stage, 'conditionB' becomes true instead, the three cache entries will persist even when one of the components has unsubscribed. If, later, only 'conditionC' is true, one of the three cache entries (for useGetUserQuery(3)) will be removed after 60s, as the subscription reference count for the cache entry has dropped to zero.

```
function ComponentOne() {
  const { data } = useGetUserQuery(1);    // component subscribes to the data
  return <div>...</div>
}
function ComponentTwo() {
  const { data } = useGetUserQuery(2);    // component subscribes to the data
  return <div>...</div>
}
function ComponentThree() {
  const { data } = useGetUserQuery(3);    // component subscribes to the data
  return <div>...</div>
}
function ComponentFour() {
  const { data } = useGetUserQuery(3);    // component subscribes to the *same* data as
                                          // ComponentThree, as it has the same query
                                          // parameters
  return <div>...</div>
}
function App(){
  ...
  if (conditionA) return (<div>
    <ComponentOne/>
    <ComponentTwo/>
    <ComponentThree/>
    <ComponentFour/>
  </div>);
  if (conditionB) return (<div>
    <ComponentOne/>
    <ComponentTwo/>
    <ComponentThree/>
  </div>);
  if (conditionC) return (<div>
    <ComponentOne/>
    <ComponentTwo/>
  </div>);
}
```

The expiration time can be configured with the **keepUnusedDataFor** property for the API definition, as well as on a per-endpoint basis:

```
import { createApi, fetchBaseQuery } from '@reduxjs/toolkit/query/react'
export const api = createApi({
  baseQuery: fetchBaseQuery({ baseUrl: '/' }),
  // global configuration for the api
  keepUnusedDataFor: 30,
  endpoints: (builder) => ({
    getPosts: builder.query({
      query: () => `posts`,
      // configuration for an individual endpoint, overriding the api setting
      keepUnusedDataFor: 5,
    }),
  }),
})
```

4.4. Refetching

After a query has been performed, you can update the associated cache entry by refetching the data from the server in several ways:

1) **Polling the server repeatedly**, eg.

```
useGetPostQuery(123,{pollingInterval:30000});
```

2) **Invalidating the cache tag assigned to the query**, as you have previously seen.

Note that you can also manually invalidate tags outside your endpoint definitions. eg.

```
dispatch(api.util.invalidateTags(['Post']))
dispatch(api.util.invalidateTags([{ type: 'Post', id: 1 }]))
dispatch(
  api.util.invalidateTags([
    { type: 'Post', id: 1 },
    { type: 'Post', id: 'LIST' },
  ])
)
```

3) **Removing all cache entries:**

```
dispatch(api.util.resetApiState())
```

4) **Manually triggering the refetch with <u>refetch()</u> and <u>initiate()</u>:**

```
import { useDispatch } from 'react-redux'
import { useGetPostsQuery } from './api'
const Component = () => {
  const dispatch = useDispatch()
  const { data, refetch } = useGetPostsQuery({ count: 5 })
  function handleRefetchOne() {
    // force re-fetches the data
    refetch()
  }
  function handleRefetchTwo() {
    // has the same effect as `refetch` for the associated query
    dispatch(
      api.endpoints.getPosts.initiate(
        { count: 5 },
        { subscribe: false, forceRefetch: true }
      )
    )
  }
  return (
    <div>
      <button onClick={handleRefetchOne}>Force re-fetch 1</button>
      <button onClick={handleRefetchTwo}>Force re-fetch 2</button>
    </div>
  )
}
```

5) Encouraging re-fetching with <u>refetchOnMountOrArgChange</u>. In addition to 'true', you can pass in a number to indicate the number of seconds that must have elapsed in order to refetch the query, when a new component mounts and subscribes to the query, or when the arguments change.

Imagine you go from usePage(1) to usePage(2) and then back to usePage(1) - all in the same component. At that point, the cache entry for page 1 could still be in the cache - and with refetchOnMountOrArgChange() you can decide at which point the cache entry is considered "too old" and a refetch would be necessary.

```
import { createApi, fetchBaseQuery } from '@reduxjs/toolkit/query/react'
export const api = createApi({
  baseQuery: fetchBaseQuery({ baseUrl: '/' }),
  // global configuration for the api
  refetchOnMountOrArgChange: 30,
  endpoints: (builder) => ({
    getPosts: builder.query({
      query: () => `posts`,
    }),
  }),
})
```

```
import { useGetPostsQuery } from './api'
const Component = () => {
  const { data } = useGetPostsQuery(
    { count: 5 },
    // this overrules the api definition setting,
    // forcing the query to always fetch when this component is mounted
    { refetchOnMountOrArgChange: true }
  )

  return ...
}
```

6) Re-fetching on window focus with <u>refetchOnFocus</u>. Note that this requires setupListeners() to have been called.

```
import { createApi, fetchBaseQuery } from '@reduxjs/toolkit/query/react'
export const api = createApi({
  baseQuery: fetchBaseQuery({ baseUrl: '/' }),
  // global configuration for the api
  refetchOnFocus: true,
  endpoints: (builder) => ({
    getPosts: builder.query({
      query: () => `posts`,
    }),
  }),
})
```

```
import { useGetPostsQuery } from './api'
const Component = () => {
  const { data } = useGetPostsQuery(
    { count: 5 },
    // this overrules the api definition setting,
    { refetchOnFocus: true }
  }
  return <div>...</div>
}
```

7) Re-fetching on network reconnection with <u>refetchOnReconnect</u>. Note that this requires setupListeners() to have been called.

```
import { createApi, fetchBaseQuery } from '@reduxjs/toolkit/query/react'
export const api = createApi({
  baseQuery: fetchBaseQuery({ baseUrl: '/' }),
  // global configuration for the api
  refetchOnReconnect: true,
  endpoints: (builder) => ({
    getPosts: builder.query({
      query: () => `posts`,
    }),
  }),
})
```

```
import { useGetPostsQuery } from './api'
const Component = () => {
  const { data } = useGetPostsQuery(
    { count: 5 },
    // this overrules the api definition setting,
    { refetchOnReconnect: true }
  }
  return <div>...</div>
}
```

4.5. Manual Cache Update

You can make changes to a cache entry directly by calling **api.util.updateQueryData()**.

Optimistic Update. ie. reflecting changes before the server responds.

```
import { createApi, fetchBaseQuery } from '@reduxjs/toolkit/query'
const api = createApi({
  baseQuery: fetchBaseQuery({
    baseUrl: '/',
  }),
  tagTypes: ['Post'],
  endpoints: (build) => ({
    getPost: build.query({
      query: (id) => `post/${id}`,
      providesTags: ['Post'],
    }),
    updatePost: build.mutation({
      query: ({ id, ...patch }) => ({
        url: `post/${id}`,
        method: 'PATCH',
        body: patch,
      }),
      async onQueryStarted({ id, ...patch }, { dispatch, queryFulfilled }) {
        const patchResult = dispatch(
          api.util.updateQueryData('getPost', id, (draft) => {
            Object.assign(draft, patch)
          })
        )
        try {
          await queryFulfilled
        } catch {
          patchResult.undo()
          /**
           * Alternatively, on failure you can invalidate the corresponding cache tags
           * to trigger a re-fetch:
           * dispatch(api.util.invalidateTags(['Post']))   <--- notice the use of another utility function
           */
        }
        // queryFulfilled.catch(patchResult.undo);    // alternative
      },
    }),
  }),
})
```

Pessimistic Update. ie. reflecting changes after the server responds.

```
import { createApi, fetchBaseQuery } from '@reduxjs/toolkit/query'
const api = createApi({
  baseQuery: fetchBaseQuery({
    baseUrl: '/',
  }),
  tagTypes: ['Post'],
  endpoints: (build) => ({
    getPost: build.query({
      query: (id) => `post/${id}`,
      providesTags: ['Post'],
    }),
    updatePost: build.mutation({
      query: ({ id, ...patch }) => ({
        url: `post/${id}`,
        method: 'PATCH',
        body: patch,
      }),
      async onQueryStarted({ id, ...patch }, { dispatch, queryFulfilled }) {
        try {
          const { data: updatedPost } = await queryFulfilled
          const patchResult = dispatch(
            api.util.updateQueryData('getPost', id, (draft) => {
              Object.assign(draft, updatedPost)
            })
          )
        } catch {}
      },
    }),
  }),
})
```

General Update

```
import { api } from './api'
import { useAppDispatch } from './store/hooks'
function App() {
  const dispatch = useAppDispatch()
  function handleClick() {
    /**
     * This will update the cache data for the query corresponding to the `getPosts` endpoint,
     * when that endpoint is used with no argument (undefined).
     */
    const patchCollection = dispatch(
      api.util.updateQueryData('getPosts', undefined, (draftPosts) => {
        draftPosts.push({ id: 1, name: 'Teddy' })
      })
    )
  }
  return <button onClick={handleClick}>Add post to cache</button>
}
```

If you want to merge a JSON diff/patch array with the cached data, instead of completely replacing the old entry, you can use **api.util.patchQueryData()** instead.

```
const patchCollection = dispatch(
  api.util.updateQueryData('getPosts', undefined, (draftPosts) => {
    draftPosts.push({ id: 1, name: 'Teddy' })
  })
)
...
dispatch(
  api.util.patchQueryData('getPosts', undefined, patchCollection.inversePatches)
)
...
patchCollection.undo()
```

4.6. Conditional Rendering

You can prevent the automatic fetching of a query by setting the **skip** option to true in a query hook.

Redux Toolkit Query also supports the use of Typescript.
(see official example at: https://codesandbox.io/s/github/reduxjs/ redux-toolkit/tree/master/examples/query/react/conditional-fetching)

4.7. Prefetching

Using the **usePrefetch()** hook, you can prefetch some data to the cache for a page before the user navigates to the page or attempts to load some known content.

If the query exists in the cache, and
- no options are specified, OR
- *ifOlderThan* evaluates to false,

the query will not be performed.

If *ifOlderThan* evaluates to true, the query will be performed even if there is an existing cache entry.

```
function User() {
  const prefetchUser = usePrefetch('getUser')
  // Low priority hover will not fire unless the last request happened more than 35s ago
  // High priority hover will always fire
  return (
    <div>
      <button onMouseEnter={() => prefetchUser(4, { ifOlderThan: 35 })}>
        Low priority
      </button>
      <button onMouseEnter={() => prefetchUser(4, { force: true })}>
        High priority
      </button>
    </div>
  );
}
```

Alternatively, you can do the following to prefetch data:

```
store.dispatch(
  api.util.prefetch(endpointName, arg, { force: false, ifOlderThan: 10 })
)
dispatch(api.endpoints[endpointName].initiate(arg, { forceRefetch: true }))
```

Eg. prefetching the next page in advance...

```
const PostList = () => {
  const [page, setPage] = useState(1)
  const { data: posts, isLoading, isFetching } = useListPostsQuery(page)
  const prefetchPage = usePrefetch('listPosts')

  const prefetchNext = useCallback(() => {
    prefetchPage(page + 1)
  }, [prefetchPage, page])

  useEffect(() => {
    if (page !== posts?.total_pages) {
      prefetchNext()
    }
  }, [posts, page, prefetchNext])

  if (isLoading) {
    return <div>Loading</div>
  }

  if (!posts?.data) {
    return <div>No posts :(</div>
  }
```

```
return (
  <Box>
    <HStack spacing="14px">
      <Button
        onClick={() => setPage((prev) => prev - 1)}
        isLoading={isFetching}
        disabled={page === 1}
      >
        <Icon as={MdArrowBack} />
      </Button>
      <Button
        onClick={() => setPage((prev) => prev + 1)}
        isLoading={isFetching}
        disabled={page === posts.total_pages}
        onMouseEnter={prefetchNext}
      >
        <Icon as={MdArrowForward} />
      </Button>
      <Box>{`${page} / ${posts.total_pages}`}</Box>
    </HStack>
    <List spacing={3} mt={6}>
      {posts?.data.map(({ id, title, status }) => (
        <ListItem key={id}>
          <ListIcon as={MdBook} color="green.500" /> {title}{' '}
          <Badge
            ml="1"
            fontSize="0.8em"
            colorScheme={getColorForStatus(status)}
          >
            {status}
          </Badge>
        </ListItem>
      ))}
    </List>
  </Box>
)
}
```

4.8. Customizing Cache Keys

By default, when creating a cache entry, RTK Query will take the query arguments, sort object keys where applicable, stringify the result, and concatenate it with the endpoint name. This creates a cache key based on the combination of arguments + endpoint name (ignoring object key order), such that calling any given endpoint with the same arguments will result in the same cache key.

Thus, calling *useGetPostQuery({id:1,user:'moon'})*
after *useGetPostQuery({user:'moon', id:1})* will not cause a refetch.

Sometimes, you may want to map different queries to the same cache key. To do that, you can define your own mapping function for the cache keys
with ***serializeQueryArgs***:

```
export const postApi = createApi({
  reducerPath: "postApi",
  baseQuery: fetchBaseQuery({ baseUrl: "https://webcodingcenter.com/shared/" }),
  endpoints: (builder) => ({
   getPost: builder.query({
     query: (id) => `get_post.php?id=${id}`
   })
 }),
  serializeQueryArgs: q => (q.endpointName+Math.floor(q.queryArgs/3))
                           // <-- define this function to customize cache keys
});
```

4.9. Code Splitting

After you have setup your initial service definition:
(eg.)

```
export const emptySplitApi = createApi({
  baseQuery: fetchBaseQuery({ baseUrl: '/' }),
  endpoints: () => ({}),
})
```

You can inject endpoints at a later stage with *injectEndpoints()*:
(eg.)

```
const extendedApi = emptySplitApi.injectEndpoints({
  endpoints: (build) => ({
    example: build.query({
      query: () => 'test',
    }),
  }),
  overrideExisting: false,
})
```

For larger applications that may have many endpoints, this can be beneficial, allowing you to trim down your initial bundle size.

The individual API slice endpoint definitions can also be split across multiple files. This is primarily useful for working with API slices that were code-generated from an API schema file, allowing you to add additional custom behavior and configuration to a set of automatically-generated endpoint definitions.

If you already have existing endpoint definitions, and want to merge them together on a per-definition basis with new definitions (ie. *Object.assign(existingEndpoint, newPartialEndpoint)*), you can use *enhanceEndpoints()* instead.

```
const enhancedApi = api.enhanceEndpoints({
  addTagTypes: ['User'],
  endpoints: {
    getUserByUserId: {
      providesTags: ['User'],
    },
    patchUserByUserId: {
      invalidatesTags: ['User'],
    },
    // alternatively, define a function which is called with the endpoint definition as an argument
    getUsers(endpoint) {
      endpoint.providesTags = ['User']
      endpoint.keepUnusedDataFor = 120
    },
  },
})
```

Nothing will happen with enhanceEndpoints() if the endpoints did not exist before.

4.10. Action Matchers

There exists a set of Redux Toolkit action matching utilities that match the pending, fulfilled, and rejected actions that will be dispatched by this thunk. These allow you to match on Redux actions for that endpoint, such as in createSlice.extraReducers or a custom middleware. Those are implemented as follows:

```
api.endpoints.x.matchPending    // isAllOf(isPending(thunk), matchesEndpoint(endpoint)),
api.endpoints.x.matchFulfilled  // isAllOf(isFulfilled(thunk), matchesEndpoint(endpoint)),
api.endpoints.x.matchRejected   // isAllOf(isRejected(thunk), matchesEndpoint(endpoint)),
```

4.11. Server-Side Rendering

TK Query supports Server Side Rendering (SSR) with _**Next.js**_ via rehydration with next-redux-wrapper.

You should, in getStaticProps or getServerSideProps:
- Pre-fetch all queries via the initiate actions,
  e.g. store.dispatch(api.endpoints.getPokemonByName.initiate(name))
- Wait for each query to finish using await
  Promise.all(api.util.getRunningOperationPromises())

```
import { createApi, fetchBaseQuery } from '@reduxjs/toolkit/query/react'
import { HYDRATE } from 'next-redux-wrapper'

export const api = createApi({
  baseQuery: fetchBaseQuery({ baseUrl: '/' }),
  extractRehydrationInfo(action, { reducerPath }) {
    if (action.type === HYDRATE) {
      return action.payload[reducerPath]
    }
  },
  endpoints: (build) => ({
  // omitted
  }),
})
```

If you are not using Next.js, you should define another version of createApi({}):

```
import {
  buildCreateApi,
  coreModule,
  reactHooksModule,
} from '@reduxjs/toolkit/query/react'

const createApi = buildCreateApi(
  coreModule(),
  reactHooksModule({ unstable__sideEffectsInRender: true })
)
```

...and wait for all queries to finish using await Promise.all(api.util.getRunningOperationPromises()) before performing the next render cycle.

API state rehydration can be used in conjunction with Redux Persist by leveraging the REHYDRATE action type imported from redux-persist. This can be used out of the box with the autoMergeLevel1 or autoMergeLevel2 state reconcilers when persisting the root reducer, or with the autoMergeLevel1 reconciler when persisting just the api reducer.

```
import { createApi, fetchBaseQuery } from '@reduxjs/toolkit/query/react'
import { REHYDRATE } from 'redux-persist'

export const api = createApi({
  baseQuery: fetchBaseQuery({ baseUrl: '/' }),
  extractRehydrationInfo(action, { reducerPath }) {
    if (action.type === REHYDRATE) {
      return action.payload[reducerPath]
    }
  },
  endpoints: (build) => ({
    // omitted
  }),
})
```

4.12. Miscellaneous APIs
1. buildCreateApi(), coreModule, etc.

If you want to use different versions of useSelector or useDispatch for a custom context, you can do the following:

```
import * as React from 'react'
import { createDispatchHook } from 'react-redux'
import {
  buildCreateApi,
  coreModule,
  reactHooksModule,
} from '@reduxjs/toolkit/query/react'

const MyContext = React.createContext(null)
const customCreateApi = buildCreateApi(
  coreModule(),
  reactHooksModule({ useDispatch: createDispatchHook(MyContext) })
)
```

If you want to create your own module, you should review the react-hooks module to see what an implementation would look like:

```
import { CoreModule } from '@internal/core/module'
import {
  BaseQueryFn,
  EndpointDefinitions,
  Api,
  Module,
  buildCreateApi,
  coreModule,
} from '@reduxjs/toolkit/query'

export const customModuleName = Symbol()
export type CustomModule = typeof customModuleName

declare module '../apiTypes' {
  export interface ApiModules<
    BaseQuery extends BaseQueryFn,
    Definitions extends EndpointDefinitions,
    ReducerPath extends string,
    TagTypes extends string
  > {
    [customModuleName]: {
      endpoints: {
        [K in keyof Definitions]: {
          myEndpointProperty: string
        }
      }
    }
  }
}

export const myModule = (): Module => ({
  name: customModuleName,
  init(api, options, context) {
    // initialize stuff here if you need to

    return {
      injectEndpoint(endpoint, definition) {
        const anyApi = (api as any) as Api<
          any,
          Record,
          string,
          string,
          CustomModule | CoreModule
        >
        anyApi.endpoints[endpoint].myEndpointProperty = 'test'
      },
    }
  },
})

export const myCreateApi = buildCreateApi(coreModule(), myModule())
```

2. baseQuery

Instead of using fetchBaseQuery(), you can define your own base query. eg.:

```
const customBaseQuery = (
  args,
  { signal, dispatch, getState },
  extraOptions
) => {
  if (Math.random() > 0.5) return { error: 'Too high!' }
  return { data: 'All good!' }
}
```

You can use <u>Axios</u>:

```
import { createApi } from '@reduxjs/toolkit/query'
import axios from 'axios'

const axiosBaseQuery = ({ baseUrl } = { baseUrl: '' }) => async ({ url, method, data, params })
=> {
  try {
    const result = await axios({ url: baseUrl + url, method, data, params })
    return { data: result.data }
  } catch (axiosError) {
    let err = axiosError
    return {
      error: {
        status: err.response?.status,
        data: err.response?.data || err.message,
      },
    }
  }
}

const api = createApi({
  baseQuery: axiosBaseQuery({baseUrl: 'https://example.com'}),
  endpoints(build) {
    return {
      query: build.query({ query: () => ({ url: '/query', method: 'get' }) }),
      mutation: build.mutation({
        query: () => ({ url: '/mutation', method: 'post' }),
      }),
    }
  },
})
```

You can use GraphQL:

```
import { createApi } from '@reduxjs/toolkit/query'
import { request, gql, ClientError } from 'graphql-request'

const graphqlBaseQuery =
  ({ baseUrl }) =>
  async ({ body }) => {
    try {
      const result = await request(baseUrl, body)
      return { data: result }
    } catch (error) {
      if (error instanceof ClientError) {
        return { error: { status: error.response.status, data: error } }
      }
      return { error: { status: 500, data: error } }
    }
  }

export const api = createApi({
  baseQuery: graphqlBaseQuery({
    baseUrl: 'https://graphqlzero.almansi.me/api',
  }),
  endpoints: (builder) => ({
    getPosts: builder.query({
      query: () => ({
        body: gql`
        query {
          posts {
            data {
              id
              title
            }
          }
        }
        `,
      }),
      transformResponse: (response) => response.posts.data,
    }),
    getPost: builder.query({
      query: (id) => ({
        body: gql`
        query {
          post(id: ${id}) {
            id
            title
            body
          }
        }
        `,
      }),
      transformResponse: (response) => response.post,
    }),
  }),
})
```

You can wrap fetchBaseQuery() such that when encountering a *401 Unauthorized error*, an additional request is sent to refresh an authorization token, and re-try to initiate query after re-authorizing.

```
import { fetchBaseQuery } from '@reduxjs/toolkit/query'
import { tokenReceived, loggedOut } from './authSlice'

const baseQuery = fetchBaseQuery({ baseUrl: '/' })
const baseQueryWithReauth = async (args, api, extraOptions) => {
  let result = await baseQuery(args, api, extraOptions)
  if (result.error && result.error.status === 401) {   // try to get a new token
    const refreshResult = await baseQuery('/refreshToken', api, extraOptions)
    if (refreshResult.data) {
      api.dispatch(tokenReceived(refreshResult.data));      // store the new token
      result = await baseQuery(args, api, extraOptions);    // retry the initial query
    } else {
      api.dispatch(loggedOut())
    }
  }
  return result
}
```

You can use async-mutex to prevent multiple unauthorized errors:

```
import { fetchBaseQuery } from '@reduxjs/toolkit/query'
import { tokenReceived, loggedOut } from './authSlice'
import { Mutex } from 'async-mutex'

// create a new mutex
const mutex = new Mutex()
const baseQuery = fetchBaseQuery({ baseUrl: '/' })
const baseQueryWithReauth = async (args, api, extraOptions) => {
  // wait until the mutex is available without locking it
  await mutex.waitForUnlock()
  let result = await baseQuery(args, api, extraOptions)
  if (result.error && result.error.status === 401) {
    // checking whether the mutex is locked
    if (!mutex.isLocked()) {
      const release = await mutex.acquire()
      try {
        const refreshResult = await baseQuery(
          '/refreshToken',
          api,
          extraOptions
        )
        if (refreshResult.data) {
          api.dispatch(tokenReceived(refreshResult.data))
          // retry the initial query
          result = await baseQuery(args, api, extraOptions)
        } else {
          api.dispatch(loggedOut())
        }
      } finally {
        release();          // release must be called once the mutex should be released again.
      }
    } else {
      // wait until the mutex is available without locking it
      await mutex.waitForUnlock()
      result = await baseQuery(args, api, extraOptions)
    }
  }
  return result
}
```

RTK Query exports a utility called 'retry' that you can wrap the baseQuery with. It defaults to 5 attempts with a basic exponential backoff.
The default behavior would retry at these intervals:
  600ms * random(0.4, 1.4)
  1200ms * random(0.4, 1.4)
  2400ms * random(0.4, 1.4)
  4800ms * random(0.4, 1.4)
  9600ms * random(0.4, 1.4)

```javascript
import { createApi, fetchBaseQuery, retry } from '@reduxjs/toolkit/query/react'

// maxRetries: 5 is the default, and can be omitted. Shown for documentation purposes.
const staggeredBaseQuery = retry(fetchBaseQuery({ baseUrl: '/' }), {
  maxRetries: 5,
})
export const api = createApi({
  baseQuery: staggeredBaseQuery,
  endpoints: (build) => ({
    getPosts: build.query({
      query: () => ({ url: 'posts' }),
    }),
    getPost: build.query({
      query: (id) => ({ url: `post/${id}` }),
      extraOptions: { maxRetries: 8 }, // You can override the retry behavior on each endpoint
    }),
  }),
})

export const { useGetPostsQuery, useGetPostQuery } = api
```

```javascript
import { createApi, fetchBaseQuery, retry } from '@reduxjs/toolkit/query/react'

const staggeredBaseQueryWithBailOut = retry(
  async (args, api, extraOptions) => {
    const result = await fetchBaseQuery({ baseUrl: '/api/' })(
      args,
      api,
      extraOptions
    )

    // bail out of re-tries immediately if unauthorized,
    // because we know successive re-retries would be redundant
    if (result.error?.status === 401) {
      retry.fail(result.error)
    }

    return result
  },
  {
    maxRetries: 5,
  }
)

export const api = createApi({
  baseQuery: staggeredBaseQueryWithBailOut,
  endpoints: (build) => ({
    getPosts: build.query({
      query: () => ({ url: 'posts' }),
    }),
    getPost: build.query({
      query: (id) => ({ url: `post/${id}` }),
```

```
      extraOptions: { maxRetries: 8 }, // You can override the retry behavior on each endpoint
    }),
  }),
})
export const { useGetPostsQuery, useGetPostQuery } = api
```

In addition to 'data' and 'error', a baseQuery can also include a 'meta' property in its return value:

```
import { fetchBaseQuery, createApi } from '@reduxjs/toolkit/query'
import { uuid } from './idGenerator'

const metaBaseQuery = async (args, api, extraOptions) => {
  const requestId = uuid()
  const timestamp = Date.now()

  const baseResult = await fetchBaseQuery({ baseUrl: '/' })(
    args,
    api,
    extraOptions
  )

  return {
    ...baseResult,
    meta: baseResult.meta && { ...baseResult.meta, requestId, timestamp },
  }
}

const DAY_MS = 24 * 60 * 60 * 1000

const api = createApi({
  baseQuery: metaBaseQuery,
  endpoints: (build) => ({
    // a theoretical endpoint where we only want to return data
    // if request was performed past a certain date
    getRecentPosts: build.query({
      query: () => 'posts',
      transformResponse: (returnValue, meta) => {
        // `meta` here contains our added `requestId` & `timestamp`, as well as
        // `request` & `response` from fetchBaseQuery's meta object.
        // These properties can be used to transform the response as desired.
        if (!meta) return []
        return returnValue.filter(
          (post) => post.timestamp >= meta.timestamp - DAY_MS
        )
      },
    }),
  }),
})
```

You can construct a dynamic baseURL using a Redux state. A baseQuery has access to a getState() method that provides the current store state at the time it is called. This can be used to construct the desired url using a partial url string, and the appropriate data from your store state.

```
import { createApi, fetchBaseQuery } from '@reduxjs/toolkit/query/react'
import { selectProjectId } from './projectSlice'

const rawBaseQuery = fetchBaseQuery({
  baseUrl: 'www.my-cool-site.com/',
})

const dynamicBaseQuery = async (args, api, extraOptions) => {
  const projectId = selectProjectId(api.getState())
  // gracefully handle scenarios where data to generate the URL is missing
  if (!projectId) {
    return {
      error: {
        status: 400,
        statusText: 'Bad Request',
        data: 'No project ID received',
      },
    }
  }

  const urlEnd = typeof args === 'string' ? args : args.url
  // construct a dynamically generated portion of the url
  const adjustedUrl = `project/${projectId}/${urlEnd}`
  const adjustedArgs =
    typeof args === 'string' ? adjustedUrl : { ...args, url: adjustedUrl }
  // provide the amended url and other params to the raw base query
  return rawBaseQuery(adjustedArgs, api, extraOptions)
}

export const api = createApi({
  baseQuery: dynamicBaseQuery,
  endpoints: (builder) => ({
    getPosts: builder.query({
      query: () => 'posts',
    }),
  }),
})

export const { useGetPostsQuery } = api

/*
  Using `useGetPostsQuery()` where a `projectId` of 500 is in the redux state will result in
  a request being sent to www.my-cool-site.com/project/500/posts
*/
```

3. transformResponse

You can use transformResponse in conjunction with createEntityAdapter to normalize the data before storing it in the cache:

```
import { createApi, fetchBaseQuery } from '@reduxjs/toolkit/query/react'
import { createEntityAdapter } from '@reduxjs/toolkit'

const postsAdapter = createEntityAdapter({
  sortComparer: (a, b) => a.name.localeCompare(b.name),
})

export const api = createApi({
  baseQuery: fetchBaseQuery({ baseUrl: '/' }),
  endpoints: (build) => ({
    getPosts: build.query({
      query: () => `posts`,
      transformResponse(response, meta, arg) {
        return postsAdapter.addMany(postsAdapter.getInitialState(), response)
      },
    }),
  }),
})

export const { useGetPostsQuery } = api
```

4. queryFn
You can implement qureyFn to bypass baseQuery:

```
const queryFn = (
 args,
 { signal, dispatch, getState },
 extraOptions,
 baseQuery
) => {
 if (Math.random() > 0.5) return { error: 'Too high!' }
 return { data: 'All good!' }
}
```

Wit queryFn, you can also perform multiple requests with a single query:

```
import { createApi, fetchBaseQuery } from '@reduxjs/toolkit/query'

const api = createApi({
 baseQuery: fetchBaseQuery({ baseUrl: '/ ' }),
 endpoints: (build) => ({
  getRandomUserPosts: build.query({
   async queryFn(_arg, _queryApi, _extraOptions, fetchWithBQ) {
    // get a random user
    const randomResult = await fetchWithBQ('users/random')
    if (randomResult.error) throw randomResult.error
    const user = randomResult.data
    const result = await fetchWithBQ(`user/${user.id}/posts`)
    return result.data ? { data: result.data } : { error: result.error }
   },
  }),
 }),
})
```

Using WebSocket, you can 'stream updates':

```
import { createApi, fetchBaseQuery } from '@reduxjs/toolkit/query'

const api = createApi({
 baseQuery: fetchBaseQuery({ baseUrl: '/' }),
 tagTypes: ['Message'],
 endpoints: (build) => ({
  streamMessages: build.query({
   // The query is not relevant here as the data will be provided via streaming updates.
   // A queryFn returning an empty array is used, with contents being populated via
   // streaming updates below as they are received.
   queryFn: () => ({ data: [] }),
   async onCacheEntryAdded(arg, { updateCachedData, cacheEntryRemoved }) {
    const ws = new WebSocket('ws://localhost:8080')
    // populate the array with messages as they are received from the websocket
    ws.addEventListener('message', (event) => {
     updateCachedData((draft) => {
      draft.push(JSON.parse(event.data))
     })
    })
    await cacheEntryRemoved
    ws.close()
   },
  }),
 }),
})
```

5. <ApiProvider>

If you do not already have a Redux store, you can use this:

```
import * as React from 'react';
import { ApiProvider } from '@reduxjs/toolkit/query/react';
import { Pokemon } from './features/Pokemon';

function App() {
  return (
    <ApiProvider api={api}>
      <Pokemon />
    </ApiProvider>
  );
}
```

6. setupListeners

A utility used to enable refetchOnFocus and refetchOnReconnect behaviors. It requires the dispatch method from your store. Calling setupListeners(store.dispatch) will configure listeners with the recommended defaults, but you have the option of providing a callback for more granular control.

```
let initialized = false
export function setupListeners(
  dispatch: ThunkDispatch,
  customHandler?: (
    dispatch: ThunkDispatch,
    actions: {
      onFocus: typeof onFocus
      onFocusLost: typeof onFocusLost
      onOnline: typeof onOnline
      onOffline: typeof onOffline
    }
  ) => () => void
) {
  function defaultHandler() {
    const handleFocus = () => dispatch(onFocus())
    const handleFocusLost = () => dispatch(onFocusLost())
    const handleOnline = () => dispatch(onOnline())
    const handleOffline = () => dispatch(onOffline())
    const handleVisibilityChange = () => {
      if (window.document.visibilityState === 'visible') {
        handleFocus()
      } else {
        handleFocusLost()
      }
    }

    if (!initialized) {
      if (typeof window !== 'undefined' && window.addEventListener) {
        // Handle focus events
        window.addEventListener(
          'visibilitychange',
          handleVisibilityChange,
          false
        )
        window.addEventListener('focus', handleFocus, false)

        // Handle connection events
        window.addEventListener('online', handleOnline, false)
        window.addEventListener('offline', handleOffline, false)
        initialized = true
      }
    }
    const unsubscribe = () => {
      window.removeEventListener('focus', handleFocus)
      window.removeEventListener('visibilitychange', handleVisibilityChange)
      window.removeEventListener('online', handleOnline)
      window.removeEventListener('offline', handleOffline)
      initialized = false
    }
    return unsubscribe
  }

  return customHandler
    ? customHandler(dispatch, { onFocus, onFocusLost, onOffline, onOnline })
    : defaultHandler()
}
```

If you notice, onFocus, onFocusLost, onOffline, onOnline are all actions that are provided to the callback. Additionally, these actions are made available to api.internalActions and are able to be used by dispatching them like this:

```
dispatch(api.internalActions.onFocus())
```

5. Ecosystem

***This appendix directly adopts
https://redux.js.org/introduction/ecosystem
With due respect to the original writers, it is pointless to make changes to good
writing.

Redux is a tiny library, but its contracts and APIs are carefully chosen to spawn an
ecosystem of tools and extensions, and the community has created a wide variety
of helpful addons, libraries, and tools. You don't need to use any of these add-ons
to use Redux, but they can help make it easier to implement features and solve
problems in your application.

For an extensive catalog of libraries, add-ons, and tools related to Redux, check
out the Redux Ecosystem Links list. Also, the React/Redux Links list contains
tutorials and other useful resources for anyone learning React or Redux.

This page lists some of the Redux-related add-ons that the Redux maintainers have
vetted personally, or that have shown widespread adoption in the community.
Don't let this discourage you from trying the rest of them! The ecosystem is
growing too fast, and we have a limited time to look at everything. Consider these
the "staff picks", and don't hesitate to submit a PR if you've built something
wonderful with Redux.

5.1. Library Integration and Bindings

reduxjs/react-redux
The official React bindings for Redux, maintained by the Redux team

angular-redux/ng-redux
Angular 1 bindings for Redux

ember-redux/ember-redux
Ember bindings for Redux

glimmer-redux/glimmer-redux
Redux bindings for Ember's Glimmer component engine

tur-nr/polymer-redux
Redux bindings for Polymer

lastmjs/redux-store-element Redux bindings for custom elements

5.2. Reducers
Reducer Combination
ryo33/combineSectionReducers
An expanded version of combineReducers, which allows passing state as the third argument to all slice reducers.

KodersLab/topologically-combine-reducers
A combineReducers variation that allows defining cross-slice dependencies for ordering and data passing

```
var masterReducer = topologicallyCombineReducers(
  { auth, users, todos },
  // define the dependency tree
  { auth: ['users'], todos: ['auth'] }
)
```

Reducer Composition
acdlite/reduce-reducers
Provides sequential composition of reducers at the same level

```
const combinedReducer = combineReducers({ users, posts, comments })
const rootReducer = reduceReducers(combinedReducer, otherTopLevelFeatureReducer)
```

mhelmer/redux-xforms
A collection of composable reducer transformers

```
const createByFilter = (predicate, mapActionToKey) =>
  compose(
    withInitialState({}), // inject initial state as {}
    withFilter(predicate), // let through if action has filterName
    updateSlice(mapActionToKey), // update a single key in the state
    isolateSlice(mapActionToKey) // run the reducer on a single state slice
  )
```

adrienjt/redux-data-structures
Reducer factory functions for common data structures: counters, maps, lists (queues, stacks), sets

```
const myCounter = counter({
  incrementActionTypes: ['INCREMENT'],
  decrementActionTypes: ['DECREMENT']
})
```

Higher-Order Reducers
omnidan/redux-undo
Effortless undo/redo and action history for your reducers

omnidan/redux-ignore
Ignore redux actions by array or filter function

omnidan/redux-recycle
Reset the redux state on certain actions

ForbesLindesay/redux-optimist
A reducer enhancer to enable type-agnostic optimistic updates

5.3. Utilities
reduxjs/reselect
Creates composable memoized selector functions for efficiently deriving data from the store state

```
const taxSelector = createSelector(
  [subtotalSelector, taxPercentSelector],
  (subtotal, taxPercent) => subtotal * (taxPercent / 100)
)
```

paularmstrong/normalizr
Normalizes nested JSON according to a schema

```
const user = new schema.Entity('users')
const comment = new schema.Entity('comments', { commenter: user })
const article = new schema.Entity('articles', {
  author: user,
  comments: [comment]
})
const normalizedData = normalize(originalData, article)
```

planttheidea/selectorator
Abstractions over Reselect for common selector use cases

```
const getBarBaz = createSelector(
  ['foo.bar', 'baz'],
  (bar, baz) => `${bar} ${baz}`
)
getBarBaz({ foo: { bar: 'a' }, baz: 'b' }) // "a b"
```

5.4. Store
Change Subscriptions
jprichardson/redux-watch
Watch for state changes based on key paths or selectors

```
let w = watch(() => mySelector(store.getState()))
store.subscribe(
  w((newVal, oldVal) => {
    console.log(newval, oldVal)
  })
)
```

ashaffer/redux-subscribe
Centralized subscriptions to state changes based on paths

```
store.dispatch( subscribe("users.byId.abcd", "subscription1", () => {} );
```

Batching
tappleby/redux-batched-subscribe
Store enhancer that can debounce subscription notifications

```
const debounceNotify = _.debounce(notify => notify())
const store = configureStore({
  reducer,
  enhancers: [batchedSubscribe(debounceNotify)]
})
```

manaflair/redux-batch
Store enhancer that allows dispatching arrays of actions

```
const store = configureStore({
  reducer,
  enhancers: existingEnhancersArray => [
    reduxBatch,
    ...existingEnhancersArray,
    reduxBatch
  ]
})
store.dispatch([{ type: 'INCREMENT' }, { type: 'INCREMENT' }])
```

laysent/redux-batch-actions-enhancer
Store enhancer that accepts batched actions

```
const store = configureStore({ reducer, enhancers: [batch().enhancer] })
store.dispatch(createAction({ type: 'INCREMENT' }, { type: 'INCREMENT' }))
```

tshelburne/redux-batched-actions
Higher-order reducer that handles batched actions

```
const store = configureStore({ reducer: enableBatching(rootReducer) })
store.dispatch(batchActions([{ type: 'INCREMENT' }, { type: 'INCREMENT' }]))
```

Persistence

rt2zz/redux-persist
Persist and rehydrate a Redux store, with many extensible options

```
const persistConfig = { key: 'root', version: 1, storage }
const persistedReducer = persistReducer(persistConfig, rootReducer)
export const store = configureStore({
  reducer: persistedReducer,
  middleware: getDefaultMiddleware =>
    getDefaultMiddleware({
      serializableCheck: {
        ignoredActions: [FLUSH, REHYDRATE, PAUSE, PERSIST, PURGE, REGISTER]
      }
    })
})
export const persistor = persistStore(store)
```

react-stack/redux-storage
Persistence layer for Redux with flexible backends

```
const reducer = storage.reducer(combineReducers(reducers))
const engine = createEngineLocalStorage('my-save-key')
const storageMiddleware = storage.createMiddleware(engine)
const store = configureStore({
  reducer,
  middleware: getDefaultMiddleware =>
    getDefaultMiddleware.concat(storageMiddleware)
})
```

redux-offline/redux-offline

Persistent store for Offline-First apps, with support for optimistic UIs

```
const store = configureStore({ reducer, enhancer: [offline(offlineConfig)] })
store.dispatch({
  type: 'FOLLOW_USER_REQUEST',
  meta: { offline: { effect: {}, commit: {}, rollback: {} } }
})
```

5.5. Immutable Data

ImmerJS/immer

Immutable updates with normal mutative code, using Proxies

```
const nextState = produce(baseState, draftState => {
  draftState.push({ todo: 'Tweet about it' })
  draftState[1].done = true
})
```

5.6. Side Effects

Widely Used

reduxjs/redux-thunk

Dispatch functions, which are called and given dispatch and getState as parameters. This acts as a loophole for AJAX calls and other async behavior.

Best for: getting started, simple async and complex synchronous logic.

```
function fetchData(someValue) {
   return (dispatch, getState) => {
     dispatch({type : "REQUEST_STARTED"});

     myAjaxLib.post("/someEndpoint", {data : someValue})
        .then(response => dispatch({type : "REQUEST_SUCCEEDED", payload : response}))
        .catch(error => dispatch({type : "REQUEST_FAILED", error : error}));
   };
}

function addTodosIfAllowed(todoText) {
   return (dispatch, getState) => {
     const state = getState();

     if(state.todos.length < MAX_TODOS) {
        dispatch({type : "ADD_TODO", text : todoText});
     }
   }
}
```

listenerMiddleware (Redux Toolkit)

listenerMiddleware is intended to be a lightweight alternative to more widely used Redux async middleware like sagas and observables. While similar to thunks in the level of complexity and concept, it can be used to replicate some common saga usage patterns.

```
listenerMiddleware.startListening({
  matcher: isAnyOf(action1, action2, action3),
  effect: (action, listenerApi) => {
    const user = selectUserDetails(listenerApi.getState())

    const { specialData } = action.meta

    analyticsApi.trackUsage(action.type, user, specialData)
  }
})
```

redux-saga/redux-saga

Handle async logic using synchronous-looking generator functions. Sagas return descriptions of effects, which are executed by the saga middleware, and act like "background threads" for JS applications.

Best for: complex async logic, decoupled workflows

```
function* fetchData(action) {
  const { someValue } = action
  try {
    const response = yield call(myAjaxLib.post, '/someEndpoint', {
      data: someValue
    })
    yield put({ type: 'REQUEST_SUCCEEDED', payload: response })
  } catch (error) {
    yield put({ type: 'REQUEST_FAILED', error: error })
  }
}

function* addTodosIfAllowed(action) {
  const { todoText } = action
  const todos = yield select(state => state.todos)

  if (todos.length < MAX_TODOS) {
    yield put({ type: 'ADD_TODO', text: todoText })
  }
}
```

redux-observable/redux-observable

Handle async logic using RxJS observable chains called "epics". Compose and cancel async actions to create side effects and more.

Best for: complex async logic, decoupled workflows

```
const loginRequestEpic = action$ =>
  action$
    .ofType(LOGIN_REQUEST)
    .mergeMap(({ payload: { username, password } }) =>
     Observable.from(postLogin(username, password))
        .map(loginSuccess)
        .catch(loginFailure)
    )

const loginSuccessfulEpic = action$ =>
  action$
    .ofType(LOGIN_SUCCESS)
    .delay(2000)
    .mergeMap(({ payload: { msg } }) => showMessage(msg))

const rootEpic = combineEpics(loginRequestEpic, loginSuccessfulEpic)
```

redux-loop/redux-loop

A port of the Elm Architecture to Redux that allows you to sequence your effects naturally and purely by returning them from your reducers. Reducers now return both a state value and a side effect description.

Best for: trying to be as much like Elm as possible in Redux+JS

```
export const reducer = (state = {}, action) => {
  switch (action.type) {
    case ActionType.LOGIN_REQUEST:
      const { username, password } = action.payload
      return loop(
        { pending: true },
        Effect.promise(loginPromise, username, password)
      )
    case ActionType.LOGIN_SUCCESS:
      const { user, msg } = action.payload
      return loop(
        { pending: false, user },
        Effect.promise(delayMessagePromise, msg, 2000)
      )
    case ActionType.LOGIN_FAILURE:
      return { pending: false, err: action.payload }
    default:
      return state
  }
}
```

jeffbski/redux-logic
Side effects lib built with observables, but allows use of callbacks, promises, async/await, or observables. Provides declarative processing of actions.

Best for: very decoupled async logic

```
const loginLogic = createLogic({
  type: Actions.LOGIN_REQUEST,

  process({ getState, action }, dispatch, done) {
    const { username, password } = action.payload

    postLogin(username, password)
      .then(
        ({ user, msg }) => {
          dispatch(loginSucceeded(user))

          setTimeout(() => dispatch(showMessage(msg)), 2000)
        },
        err => dispatch(loginFailure(err))
      )
      .then(done)
  }
})
```

Promises
acdlite/redux-promise
Dispatch promises as action payloads, and have FSA-compliant actions dispatched as the promise resolves or rejects.

```
dispatch({ type: 'FETCH_DATA', payload: myAjaxLib.get('/data') })
// will dispatch either {type : "FETCH_DATA", payload : response} if resolved,
// or dispatch {type : "FETCH_DATA", payload : error, error : true} if rejected
```

lelandrichardson/redux-pack
Sensible, declarative, convention-based promise handling that guides users in a good direction without exposing the full power of dispatch.

```
dispatch({type : "FETCH_DATA", payload : myAjaxLib.get("/data") });

// in a reducer:
    case "FETCH_DATA": =
        return handle(state, action, {
            start: prevState => ({
              ...prevState,
              isLoading: true,
              fooError: null
            }),
            finish: prevState => ({ ...prevState, isLoading: false }),
            failure: prevState => ({ ...prevState, fooError: payload }),
            success: prevState => ({ ...prevState, foo: payload }),
        });
```

5.7. Middleware
Networks and Sockets
svrcekmichal/redux-axios-middleware
Fetches data with Axios and dispatches start/success/fail actions

```
export const loadCategories() => ({ type: 'LOAD', payload: { request : { url: '/categories'} } });
```

agraboso/redux-api-middleware
Reads API call actions, fetches, and dispatches FSAs

```
const fetchUsers = () => ({
  [CALL_API]: {
    endpoint: 'http://www.example.com/api/users',
    method: 'GET',
    types: ['REQUEST', 'SUCCESS', 'FAILURE']
  }
})
```

itaylor/redux-socket.io
An opinionated connector between socket.io and redux.

```
const store = configureStore({
  reducer,
  middleware: getDefaultMiddleware =>
    getDefaultMiddleware.concat(socketIoMiddleware)
})
store.dispatch({ type: 'server/hello', data: 'Hello!' })
```

tiberiuc/redux-react-firebase
Integration between Firebase, React, and Redux

Async Behavior

rt2zz/redux-action-buffer
Buffers all actions into a queue until a breaker condition is met, at which point the queue is released

wyze/redux-debounce
FSA-compliant middleware for Redux to debounce actions.

mathieudutour/redux-queue-offline
Queue actions when offline and dispatch them when getting back online.

Analytics

rangle/redux-beacon
Integrates with any analytics services, can track while offline, and decouples analytics logic from app logic

markdalgleish/redux-analytics
Watches for Flux Standard Actions with meta analytics values and processes them

5.8. Entities and Collections

tommikaikkonen/redux-orm
A simple immutable ORM to manage relational data in your Redux store.

Versent/redux-crud
Convention-based actions and reducers for CRUD logic

kwelch/entities-reducer
A higher-order reducer that handles data from Normalizr

amplitude/redux-query
Declare colocated data dependencies with your components, run queries when components mount, perform optimistic updates, and trigger server changes with Redux actions.

cantierecreativo/redux-bees
Declarative JSON-API interaction that normalizes data, with a React HOC that can run queries

GetAmbassador/redux-clerk
Async CRUD handling with normalization, optimistic updates, sync/async action creators, selectors, and an extendable reducer.

shoutem/redux-io
JSON-API abstraction with async CRUD, normalization, optimistic updates, caching, data status, and error handling.

jmeas/redux-resource
A tiny but powerful system for managing 'resources': data that is persisted to remote servers.

5.9. Component State and Encapsulation

threepointone/redux-react-local
Local component state in Redux, with handling for component actions

```
@local({
   ident: 'counter', initial: 0, reducer : (state, action) => action.me ? state + 1 : state }
})
class Counter extends React.Component {
```

epeli/lean-redux
Makes component state in Redux as easy as setState

```
const DynamicCounters = connectLean(
   scope: "dynamicCounters",
   getInitialState() => ({counterCount : 1}),
   addCounter, removeCounter
)(CounterList);
```

DataDog/redux-doghouse
Aims to make reusable components easier to build with Redux by scoping actions and reducers to a particular instance of a component.

```
const scopeableActions = new ScopedActionFactory(actionCreators)
const actionCreatorsScopedToA = scopeableActions.scope('a')
actionCreatorsScopedToA.foo('bar') //{ type: SET_FOO, value: 'bar', scopeID: 'a' }

const boundScopeableActions = bindScopedActionFactories(
  scopeableActions,
  store.dispatch
)
const scopedReducers = scopeReducers(reducers)
```

5.10. Dev Tools

Debuggers and Viewers
reduxjs/redux-devtools

Dan Abramov's original Redux DevTools implementation, built for in-app display of state and time-travel debugging

zalmoxisus/redux-devtools-extension

Mihail Diordiev's browser extension, which bundles multiple state monitor views and adds integration with the browser's own dev tools

infinitered/reactotron

A cross-platform Electron app for inspecting React and React Native apps, including app state, API requests, perf, errors, sagas, and action dispatching.

118

DevTools Monitors

Log Monitor
The default monitor for Redux DevTools with a tree view

Dock Monitor
A resizable and movable dock for Redux DevTools monitors

Slider Monitor
A custom monitor for Redux DevTools to replay recorded Redux actions

Diff Monitor
A monitor for Redux DevTools that diffs the Redux store mutations between actions

Filterable Log Monitor
Filterable tree view monitor for Redux DevTools

Filter Actions
Redux DevTools composable monitor with the ability to filter actions

Logging

evgenyrodionov/redux-logger
Logging middleware that shows actions, states, and diffs

inakianduaga/redux-state-history
Enhancer that provides time-travel and efficient action recording capabilities, including import/export of action logs and action playback.

joshwcomeau/redux-vcr
Record and replay user sessions in real-time

socialtables/redux-unhandled-action
Warns about actions that produced no state changes in development

Mutation Detection
leoasis/redux-immutable-state-invariant
Middleware that throws an error when you try to mutate your state either inside a dispatch or between dispatches.

flexport/mutation-sentinel
Helps you deeply detect mutations at runtime and enforce immutability in your codebase.

mmahalwy/redux-pure-connect
Check and log whether react-redux's connect method is passed mapState functions that create impure props.

5.11. Testing

arnaudbenard/redux-mock-store
A mock store that saves dispatched actions in an array for assertions

Workable/redux-test-belt
Extends the store API to make it easier to assert, isolate, and manipulate the store

conorhastings/redux-test-recorder
Middleware to automatically generate reducers tests based on actions in the app

wix/redux-testkit
Complete and opinionated test kit for testing Redux projects (reducers, selectors, actions, thunks)

jfairbank/redux-saga-test-plan
Makes integration and unit testing of sagas a breeze

5.12. Routing

supasate/connected-react-router Synchronize React Router v4+ state with your Redux store.

faceyspacey/redux-first-router
Seamless Redux-first routing. Think of your app in states, not routes, not components, while keeping the address bar in sync. Everything is state. Connect your components and just dispatch flux standard actions.

5.13. Forms

erikras/redux-form
A full-featured library to enable a React HTML form to store its state in Redux.

davidkpiano/react-redux-form
React Redux Form is a collection of reducer creators and action creators that make implementing even the most complex and custom forms with React and Redux simple and performant.

5.14. Higher-Level Abstractions

keajs/kea
An abstraction over Redux, Redux-Saga, and Reselect. Provides a framework for your app's actions, reducers, selectors, and sagas. It empowers Redux, making it as simple to use as setState. It reduces boilerplate and redundancy while retaining composability.

TheComfyChair/redux-scc
Takes a defined structure and uses 'behaviors' to create a set of actions, reducer responses and selectors.

Bloomca/redux-tiles
Provides minimal abstraction on top of Redux, to allow easy composability, easy async requests, and sane testability.

www.ingramcontent.com/pod-product-compliance
Lightning Source LLC
LaVergne TN
LVHW051659050326
832903LV00032B/3908